Praise for *All the Time in the World*

"*All the Time in the World* is a deep and profound exploration of who we really are and the limitless nature of our potential to create a miraculous life. Through courageously sharing her personal journey combined with her impeccable scientific research, Lisa Broderick pulls the curtain back on how we can joyfully and lovingly live in alignment with our true purpose. I highly recommend you read this book."

JACK CANFIELD
coauthor of #1 *New York Times* bestseller *Chicken Soup for the Soul*® and *The Success Principles*™

"*All the Time in the World* shows you how to have a life that's beyond what you can imagine. Anyone can benefit from the powerful insights offered in this book."

DEBRA PONEMAN
founder and CEO of Yes to Success,
award-winning speaker, and bestselling author

"One of the most profound revelations offered by the founders of quantum physics is that the material world is an illusion derived from our conscious mind, which physicists refer to as the *observer effect*. Integrating personal experiences and experiments in consciousness with frontier physics research on the observer effect, Lisa Broderick's *All the Time in the World* weaves a bridge between the realm of consciousness and the material world. Broderick's assessment of the observer effect offers a path by which thoughts, emotions, and actions shape our perceived reality.

Knowledge is power. The knowledge offered in *All the Time in the World* provides a guide for self-empowerment—an opportunity to become the creator of your world and not a victim of your fate."

BRUCE H. LIPTON, PHD
author of *New York Times* bestseller *The Biology of Belief*,
recipient of the 2009 Goi Peace Award, and distinguished researcher
emeritus at Stanford University School of Medicine

"This is a book about learning to be present in your own moment. Lisa Broderick focuses the light of modern science, especially quantum physics, on her personal near-death experience to illuminate important ideas about being the best you can be. Her mission is to coach people to get there without the extreme of going to the edge."

ROGER NELSON, PHD
prominent scientist, professor emeritus, and coordinator of
research at the Princeton Engineering Anomalies Research
(PEAR) laboratory at Princeton University

"This is an intriguing, intelligent, and important book. Its interweave of spirituality and science is breathtaking, convincing—and accessible. The narrative would, under any circumstances, push the reader forward to think about things he or she had maybe wondered about (or maybe not), but from page one feels eager to learn and understand. It is also timely in its importance, however, and significant especially for the now in which we find ourselves. As our species seems so mired in fear—from Washington, DC, to Tel Aviv and Ankara, to Beijing—Broderick's words unfold as a palliative, offering hope with an intellectual, emotional, and psychological grip to it."

ORI Z. SOLTES, PHD
professor of theology and fine arts at Georgetown University; recognized
expert on the world's religions; author of over 130 articles, essays, and
books; and director and narrator of 30 documentary videos

"This profound book is nothing short of your owner's manual for consciousness. If you are ready for healing and awakening, Lisa Broderick provides the map, tools, and protocol to open your heart and help you remember who you really are. This will not only change your life but who you are at a deep level. From here, true transformation can occur and you can accomplish anything."

"*All the Time in the World* is a guide for shifting consciousness, which, along with so many valuable tools in the world, can have as great an impact on you as on the leaders of the future!"

"This book must be read by anyone who has ever wondered about the meaning of a dream, an intuition, or life itself."

"Lisa Broderick has done an outstanding job of bringing together the wisdom of worldwide spiritual thought with an in-depth understanding of the newer quantum physics worldview. She uses these sources to explain and understand some of her very unusual experiences, which helps us to see that we may all have unlimited potential that we have not even considered. An outstanding read!"

"Lisa Broderick has given us an amazing perspective on the interplay between time, space, and an alternate reality. Her stories will certainly prompt thoughtful people to reconsider what is known and might be knowable in science, and indeed knowable by any human being."

GEORGE M. WHITE, PHD
professor of entrepreneurship at Carnegie Mellon University and
distinguished researcher emeritus at Stanford University

"A great read. It's perceptive, filled with wit, wisdom, and humor. *All the Time in the World* aggregates a lot of information from different disciplines into one understandable book. It's like a Hogwarts manual for modern times."

DAVID SANBORN
prominent entertainer who has released 24 albums, won six
Grammy Awards®, earned eight gold albums and one platinum
album, and sold over 100 million records in his career

"*All the Time in the World* is a skillfully written, carefully researched book that will motivate readers to examine the depths of their own human experience and better understand what happens as their spirituality develops beyond the physical dimension."

WILLIAM BUHLMAN
foremost expert on out-of-body travel, author of *Adventures Beyond
the Body*, and instructor at the world-famous Monroe Institute

ALL

the

TIME

in

THE

WORLD

ALL
the
TIME
in
THE
WORLD

Learn to Control Your Experience of Time
to Live a Life Without Limitations

LISA BRODERICK

sounds true
BOULDER, COLORADO

Sounds True
Boulder, CO 80306

Published 2021

Book design by Meredith March

 The wood used to produce this book is from
Forest Stewardship Council (FSC) certified forests,
recycled materials, or controlled wood.

Printed in Canada

BK06217

Library of Congress Cataloging-in-Publication Data

Names: Broderick, Lisa, author.
Title: All the time in the world : learn to control your experience of time
  to live a life without limitations / Lisa Broderick.
Description: Boulder, CO : Sounds True, 2021. | Includes bibliographical references.
Identifiers: LCCN 2020058086 (print) | LCCN 2020058087 (ebook) | ISBN
  9781683647973 (hardcover) | ISBN 9781683647980 (ebook)
Subjects: LCSH: Time perception. | Space and time. | Time–Psychological aspects.
Classification: LCC BF468 .B75 2021 (print) | LCC BF468 (ebook) | DDC
  153.7/53–dc23
LC record available at https://lccn.loc.gov/2020058086
LC ebook record available at https://lccn.loc.gov/2020058087

10 9 8 7 6 5 4 3 2 1

Contents

Foreword by don Miguel Ruiz   vii

Introduction   1

PART ONE: Update Your Construct of Time

    Chapter 1:   Time as We Know It   7

    Chapter 2:   One Part Physical: Gravity, Motion,
    and Physical Laws   17

    Chapter 3:   One Part Perception: The Quantum World   23

    Chapter 4:   How the Unseen Creates the Scene   33

    Chapter 5:   The Brainwave State of Focused Perception   43

PART TWO: Master Your Experience of Time

    Chapter 6:   Meditation: Create the State of
    Focused Perception   57

    Chapter 7:   Imagination: Experience Your Life in Advance   63

    Chapter 8:   Trauma: Reverse the Past   69

    Chapter 9:   Worry: Don't Let the Future Slow You Down   77

Contents

Chapter 10: Focus: Stretch Time   83

Chapter 11: Thoughts: Receive Insight When You Need It   89

Chapter 12: Telepathy: Reach Others Fast   93

Chapter 13: Supersight: Instantly Verify What Matters Most   99

Chapter 14: Love: Harness Metaphysical Gravity   105

Chapter 15: Death: Never Run Out of Time   111

Chapter 16: Immortality: Transcend Time   117

Chapter 17: A Suggested Daily Practice for
            Transcending Time   123

Conclusion   127

Acknowledgments   129

Appendix A: Additional Science   131

Appendix B: A Compilation of Practices   139

Notes   153

About the Author   171

Foreword
by don Miguel Ruiz

I have been writing about how to help people better know who they are for over forty years. It has been my privilege to have books published and to speak with so many people whose lives are now transformed.

But it was only recently, following one of my near-death experiences, that I became interested in helping people understand not only *who* they are but *what* they are. Because, as Lisa Broderick describes in her book *All the Time in the World*, when we truly understand what we are, we can find the source of our own exceptional power. Then we can live a fulfilled life and are free.

Based on Lisa's experiences, some of which relate to her own near-death experience, she has been able to say what many other people would put out of their mind and try never to think about again. By writing down and keeping logs of her experiences and examining them as a doctor or scientist would, Lisa has brought to the world thoughtful, clear explanations of many things. She is able to describe what happens to us as we create the reality of our lives here on Earth, where we come from, and what we can ultimately become when we overcome our own fear. I have said in my books that it is not death that is the biggest fear for humans; the biggest fear is to be alive where we take the risk to express what we really are.

When I experienced my second near-death encounter, a heart attack in 2002, I was intrigued by what was happening. For me, I was given the greatest opportunity to share with everyone how to let go of the body, how to detach from the body.

I knew to share these things because this was not my first such experience. In the late 1970s, I was driving a Volkswagen, and I made the mistake that many people do; I had drunk too much. I used to be a medical student and was close to graduation. I was outside of Mexico City, and being drunk, decided to drive back to Mexico City—a very bad decision.

Suddenly the car went out of control and directly into a concrete wall and was totaled. But incredibly, I saw the whole experience, and I saw my own body at the wheel. At that moment, I knew without a doubt that I was not in my physical body.

Before the crash, I had heard about the idea that I wasn't my physical body, but from that moment of the crash on, it was no longer a theory. For me, it was a fact.

During the crash, I was watching my body as the car crashed. I was *inside* the car, yet I was *outside* my physical body. Time was subjective. Everything was so slow that I had time to do whatever I thought about doing. I was able to surround my body in order to protect it before the crash was over, and nothing happened to my body during the crash. I did not travel further; I remained unconscious until my body woke up.

What happened after the accident was that my whole personality changed. The way I perceived life was completely different because before that accident, everything was so important, and after the accident, I saw everything as irrelevant. I began to study ancient ancestral wisdom, first with my mother who was a healer and later from a shaman in the Mexican desert.

In my career, I had already followed a family tradition. All of my brothers are doctors. One is a neurosurgeon; the other is an oncology surgeon. So I followed their steps, and I also became a surgeon. I continued to study. I graduated, and I started working, but I had a lot of questions.

My mind wanted to understand *why*. Because the first question was, well, What am I? Because I am not the physical body; that's obvious. It's obvious that I am not my identity; I am not what I believe I am. I didn't know what I was, and that really scared me. You know, I see many other people who have the same kind of near-death experience, and they start denying what happened. They just let go, and they adapt to the life they feel they cannot change.

Well, I went exactly in the opposite direction. I really wanted to know. And even when I graduated and was part of my brother's team as a surgeon, I was very interested to see how the mind works. Because for me, there was obviously a separation between the body, the mind, and what I really am. I really wanted to understand the mind because I thought I understood the body completely, and the body is matter. But the mind is not matter, which Lisa writes about in this book.

As a doctor, I did a lot of neurosurgery. It was a great time, but at a certain moment, what I discovered is that most of the people create their own physical problems with their mind. With that realization, I became very interested to understand the human mind. So I decided to change the direction of my career and not necessarily live medicine. I have followed the other tradition of my family, which is the Toltec tradition. The word "Toltec" means artist. When I talk about Toltec, I'm really talking about the entire humanity, because we all are artists.

As artists, the biggest creation we make is the story of our lives. Often in our stories, nobody abuses us more than we abuse ourselves by doubting ourselves and feeding our brain with negativity and limited beliefs. People don't like their life, so they live in a state of inaction where they are afraid to be alive. All of this is because they are creating their life through their thoughts.

In the meantime, our brain is processing all that we perceive every moment. Brains are dependent on knowledge and the need to understand. This makes the physical part of us controlled by our brain afraid of anything that it doesn't understand. This is the main reason why we are so afraid of the unknown, especially of death—because we don't understand what happens after the body dies.

Lisa explains that because reality is solely a result of who we are, our fears combined with the stories told over and over in our mind become our creation; they become our life. This is what she calls the *observer effect* from modern science.

Only when we un-limit our brain to new ways of thinking and perceiving the world around us does our physical brain become no longer afraid and our stories are cured.

The way to begin is to be impeccable with our words, because our words are the expression of our thoughts. They have the same power as thoughts to affect ourselves and others—to generate our reality.

This also means that we must take action and, by doing that, express what we are. In my book *The Four Agreements*, I write that action is about living fully. You can have many great ideas, but without action upon that idea, there will be no manifestation, no results, and no reward. In action, we are led to the source of our own power.

And that source can be found when we love ourselves. When we do that, we express that love in our interactions with others and get back what we express. In this way, it is the same as the energy coming off us that Lisa describes. If I love you, then you will love me. If I insult you, you will insult me.

When we truly love ourselves, we can accept ourselves and keep our agreements with ourselves. Then the big creation we will make will be the story of our life fulfilled and free.

The truth is we don't know what will happen tomorrow. We just have the present moment to be alive in what Lisa calls the Now. By reading this book, we learn that the gift is to accept this truth and to embrace it.

When we do that, we will be able to live as if this is the only day of our life. We can plan to live forever without being concerned about whether or not our plan will manifest. What exists is only this Now moment, and it is the source for an exceptional life. Are you ready to learn how to tap into this for yourself? By the time you are done reading *All the Time in the World*, you will be doing that and more.

Introduction

Any sufficiently advanced technology is
indistinguishable from magic.

ARTHUR C. CLARKE

In this book you will find a definitive account of how time works so you can learn to affect it for yourself.

This is not science fiction. This is science. Long ago Einstein proved that time is stretchable, like a rubber band. Ordinary humans are slowing down and speeding up time every day, often without realizing it.

What if you could slow down time? What if you could stretch and bend time for yourself?

Basic science teaches us that time forever marches forward, without fail. We view the unfolding of our lives as a linear reality, where we are at the mercy of events mostly beyond our control.

But there is another way to experience time. There is something that defies the physical law of cause and effect on which science relies to explain time. Scientists call it quantum theory. Using the principles of quantum mechanics, we can view the human construct of time in a different way, where time is less limited than we thought. We can lead lives where pretty much anything can happen. Lives free from limitation.

And so, while this book is about time, it is also about the nature of reality explained through the lens of what science is discovering about time. By posing questions like *Where do thoughts come from?* and *How do we know what is real?* we can begin to appreciate that time and reality are merely perceptions. We pretend that clockfaces show us what is real, but they don't. We continue to pretend because once we pull the thread on our human construct of time, then everything else about reality unravels, including matter, the world, the universe—everything. When we stop pretending that time is a real thing, we can access the past and the future at any moment. This state is characterized by certain brainwaves and has been called the zone, flow, and the Now. It is what I call focused perception. In this state, you can time travel anywhere you want: you may find yourself affecting the past, influencing the future, and choosing how you experience the present. In some sense, all personal transformation work is rooted in time. When we master time, we master ourselves.

You can get there by understanding the science of time. Once you know the science behind time, you will understand that our experience of time is one part physical and one part perception. The physical part of time is rooted in the science of Einstein, gravity, and relativity. The perception part of time is best explained by the principles of quantum physics. This is my theory for how time works, which you might call a "theory of everything" for time.

While awake and going through our daily lives, we each exist in a physical reality that is sometimes at odds with our perceptions. Everyone has experienced those weird coincidences, those impossible-to-explain incidents, those ". . . did I really just see that?" double takes. Recent discoveries suggest that our perceptions may be every bit as important as our physical reality.

By changing the part that you can control—your perception—you can change your experience of time. Think of it: you could intentionally step out of linear time to shift your thoughts to another time when something you want has already happened or something you want to have happen hasn't occurred yet.

As you begin to use the practices in this book, such as slowing down time and reversing the past, you'll develop your ability to time travel through your perceptions. These practices will fuel your mind, stimulate your brain to generate ideas and solutions, and become an endless source of inspiration, intuition, insight, and innovation. Your physical reality and your perception will meld into a more fluid, unified reality, allowing you to change your experience of time—and your ability to do what is yours to do.

Before she died a few years ago, I asked my mother, a clinically minded person trained as an economist, why people read self-help books. Her answer: people want to know why things happened to them. I found that answer very insightful.

I later realized that not only do people want to know why things happened to them (in the past), they want to influence what will happen to them so they can create what they want (in the future). This means that our ability to influence our experience of time is also key to creating the reality we desire.

An early childhood accident, which you will read more about in chapter 1, forever changed my understanding of time and space and gave me the ability to see things in a nonlinear fashion. A kind of curtain was lifted, and I saw a world influenced by subtleties, including our own thoughts, feelings, and imagination. As a result, I sensed more, intuited more, and saw more. People like this used to be called mystics. That no longer has to be the case. Experiences like mine are for everyone.

My intention in writing this book was to give others an opportunity to stumble over the truth as I have. The question is, What will you do next? You could choose to just ignore all of this and go on like nothing happened. Or you could allow what is contained in these pages to inspire a new practice, a new perception, a new way of life. Changing your experience of time is both theoretically and practically possible—and has been my own personal life experience. It has also been the experience of many others, whose personal, real-life stories you will read in this book. It can also be yours.

If you feel that the seconds are slipping through your fingers and there is nothing you can do about it, *All the Time in the World* will liberate you from the illusion that time is your enemy. Instead, like so many whose stories are shared in this book, you can use time as an ally as you become a confident creator of your own reality. You have all the time in the world.

PART ONE

Update Your Construct of Time

1

Time as
We Know It

Let's take a brief look at life in these times. Before the pandemic of 2020, many of us felt overwhelmed by the pace of life. As an interested friend offering advice, I noticed that regardless of background or current circumstances, most people seemed to have the same core issue: they didn't have enough time to do what they needed to do.

And no wonder. Our devices bombarded us with information, making us feel like we couldn't possibly keep up with it all. Much of this information was unimportant news or marketing messages, so we didn't even know *how* to know what was true, much less what to act on. Every week we heard of a new mass shooting or record-breaking natural disaster. Paradigms were shifting in virtually every discipline, from physics to medicine to culture and beyond.

Then the pandemic hit. The same people overwhelmed by the busyness of life just a few short months prior were now under stay-at-home orders, unable to engage in their usual routines of shopping, work, socializing, school, and commuting.

During the early months of the pandemic, I often asked people about their experiences of time and if it had changed for them. "Yes" was the nearly universal answer. Before the pandemic, time had seemed to move at lightning speed. Now, some said, time passed so slowly that every day felt like a week. Others said time seemed to pass in a blur, so that the months-long episode felt like the same long day. Still others said both felt true: every day felt like a week, yet the weeks sped by like days.

Although mostly grateful for being able to spend so much time at home (at first), people were also confused. Why did time seem to behave so oddly?

My answer was this: time is not what you think.

Whether we can't get enough of it or it can't pass quickly enough, time is the one problem that still unites us all. It's often described as the world's only nonrenewable resource: once it's gone, it's gone, and there's nothing we can do to change that.

Or is there?

My own experience of time changed dramatically around the age of four or five, when I experienced a nearly fatal fall through a plate-glass window. Our family was vacationing in a cabin in Northern Arizona, and my younger sister and I were playing together by jumping on and between two twin beds. At one point, I jumped too close to the edge of the bed, and as it slid out from beneath my feet, I was hurled through the window. My mother remembered seeing me fly through the air in slow motion. I broke the window with my head and landed half inside, half outside, with the severed glass from the bottom pane still inside of me. Before taking me to the nearest doctor, which as I recall was a country facility miles away, my mother was told by a doctor who happened to be at the scene, "I don't think she's going to make it."

While I don't recall that conversation, I do remember much of the experience even though I had lost consciousness. I recall being on the windowpane and being loaded into the back door of our station wagon. I remember the drive through the country to the doctor's office. Most clearly, I remember the room I was in while being operated on. I remember looking down from above where my body would have been. I don't have a clear memory of my body or the actual operation, but I recall looking out a window beyond a metal cabinet to my right where supplies seemed to be stored. When we returned home to Phoenix, I recall being in a cast for months, from my waist to my armpits.

I eventually recovered and was once again a little girl full of life. But the way I saw the world had changed forever. I thought of everything around me as connected, alive, and conscious. I used to imagine I had superpowers that I could use to slow down clockfaces, having had many experiences of "the zone," which athletes describe as a transcendent experience where they experience slowed-down time. While bowling, running, or doing other similar activities, time would seem to slow down so I could perform at a heightened level that wasn't typical for me. Today, we know "the zone" is the key to peak performance and experiencing our highest potential. For me, these experiences made me feel that I was more than an average kid. It turns out I may have been right.

Around the age of eight, I remember bowling with my older brother. We were in a league where we bowled fairly often, but I wasn't good at it. One evening, though, I remember bowling a nearly perfect game. Surprisingly to say the least, it seemed as though any ball I rolled down the lane ended up as a strike, no matter how carelessly I threw it. I recall seeing whether I could intentionally mess up and aim the ball at other lanes just to see what would happen. Strike after strike occurred until the last few bowls when, in shock and exasperation, I didn't bowl strikes and instead bowled something more like spares. All of this occurred while I was experiencing a sense of timelessness during what was clearly a transcendent experience.

Later on, I felt I could easily slow down time and often practiced doing it, arriving at destinations seemingly too early to have physically walked or driven there. Many years ago in high school, I needed to take one of the Scholastic Aptitude Tests (SAT) for admission to college. I was running late the morning of the test and left for my high school, about thirty miles away over a mountain pass, less than thirty minutes prior to the start time—too late in my experience to arrive before the doors closed. Instead of worrying about being late, though, I focused on being seated at a desk precisely on time. I got in my car and played the movie of myself walking through the door with the wall-mounted clockface displaying the precise time I needed it to be. I later walked through the school doors into the room and sat down right on time for the test.

In all of these cases, I rarely told anyone, too uncomfortable to share these stories with my family or friends because I thought they might judge me as weird or crazy. At times, as a child, I would bring up some miraculous event, such as feeling like I had flown or that time had stopped. But grown-ups around me called it magical thinking, which often happens in the minds of children. Moreover, memory is a problematic thing. There is no way to know what really happened as individual memories naturally get changed, duplicated, and distorted over time.

Even so, I wanted to understand why my experiences of time seemed different from others around me. After a decades-long search through ancient texts, mystery schools, and esoteric spiritual practices, I discovered that what I recall being my experiences were neither new nor unusual: ancient Eastern spiritual traditions had been teaching their practitioners to do exactly what I had stumbled upon for thousands of years.

Being a Westerner, however, I wanted to understand how these experiences were possible based on science and data. My quest ultimately led me to modern science, where the language of physics helped explain what I experienced over so many years. This is what I know and have discovered from science: Time is one part physical and one part perception, which explains why it sometimes seems stretchable like a rubber band. Experienced time is controlled, in part, by you.

The secret is improving your skill of what I call *focused perception*. Focused perception is a heightened state of awareness that can happen to a person in a lot of different contexts: including playing a sport, experiencing grave danger, or bringing it on intentionally through the practices I outline in this book. It is a state of perception where someone might feel deep concentration, a sense of mastery, a lack of self-consciousness, and self-transcendence. It is also a special experience where time does not pass as usual and typically slows down or seems to completely stop. Discovering how to bring on this state for yourself allows you to finally transcend time.

You may have already experienced the kind of focused perception that results in strange experiences of time. Years ago, my friend Bill described to me how he was driving on a California highway at about eighty miles an hour with the traffic. In the lane to his left, he saw a woman in a car going the same speed as he was. In front of him, he saw a large tire fall off the back of a truck, bounce three times, go through her windshield, and kill her, all in slow motion. Meanwhile, according to his perception, he had all the time in the world to do what needed to be done. While the other vehicle was slowly spinning out of control, Bill maneuvered to the side of the road and avoided a collision. His experience of the life-threatening nature of the moment seemed to cause time to slow down dramatically for him, to the point where he could save his own life.

Perhaps time has seemed to stand still for you during a similar experience of danger or while you were lost in a wonderful memory, watching the waves at the beach, holding your newborn, or in the flow of your work.

In each of these cases, this state of focused perception produced feelings of transcending time. What do I mean by transcending time? It is a state often characterized by deep concentration, emotional buoyancy, a sense of mastery, a lack of self-consciousness, and a sense of self-transcendence. Many people call this experience "the zone," "flow," "the Now," "being in the present moment," or simply "presence."

Usually we have these experiences spontaneously, triggered perhaps by certain circumstances like a near-death experience (like I had), extreme danger (like Bill), extreme love (a spiritual epiphany or holding your newborn), or extreme focus (like on the basketball court). But rather than waiting for these experiences to happen unpredictably in moments of danger or when lost in thought, I'm going to show you how to create this sense of transcending time at will. The way to do it is to change the part of the time equation you control: your own perception. Through simple practices anyone can learn, you can finally transcend clockfaces and your outdated construct of time.

Regardless of what someone thinks their issue is, I've found that changing their construct of time unlocks personal transformation—allowing them to make a "quantum leap" forward in nearly every area of their lives. If time is *not* forever uniformly moving forward, what if we can stretch and bend it enough to suit our personal needs? What if we are able to change our experience of how time passes in the physical world—without building a time machine?

I met a woman a few years ago at a conference full of fascinating and successful people. She herself was highly accomplished in her career.

We struck up a conversation, and she told me that she felt frustrated. She sensed the dreams of her future were hampered by memories of her past, and she felt stuck.

Based on principles you will learn in this book, I showed her how time doesn't exist in the way she had perceived her whole life. Time is not linear and fixed, but stretchable—something she could interact with and even control. I explained how, if she knew the science behind time, she could affect time for herself. And while my work with her was about transcending clockfaces, it was also about personal transformation. If she continued to squander moments of time paralyzed by regrets from the past and fear of the future, then no amount of stopped clockfaces would enable her to do what she wanted to do.

I shared with her two specific practices that allowed her to change her perception of both her past and her future so she could create what she wanted in her life. It took practice and focus, but she mentally awakened to the point where it became possible for her to move beyond her past and begin to master the way the world works in deep and meaningful ways.

Did it help her? Here's how she put it:

> Using the practices that Lisa taught me has transformed my life. The things that had blocked me in my life have lost their power. The goals that had seemed distant are now very much at hand. And the tool of focused perception has made me so much more productive in my work; I have found that focused perception is the inverse of panic. It slows time, and free of stress, I am free to accomplish goals—and more of them!
>
> Focused perception has made me a better athlete as well. I play tennis. The more I focus on the ball coming toward me from the other side of the net, the more time I have to ready myself for it and to connect. Also, the more focused I am on the ball, the more relaxed I am. I feel I have all the time necessary to hit the ball well. This practical application serves to remind me that I have all the time necessary in any area of my life.

I was lucky. I met Lisa at a time when I sensed that conscious-ness was the answer to all of my problems, but it was Lisa who handed me the key to its uses.

She changed her perception of time. She realized she is not bound to time, but a creator of it, and truly has all the time in the world to do everything she wants to do. She also has practical tools and strategies to ensure things happen at the right time, which results in a deep sense of connectedness and abundance. She is on her way to transcending time.

With all the effort we put into managing time, we have to ask: Why is the issue of time so important to us anyway? I believe one reason is that we want to know the answer to this fundamental question: What is mine to do, *now*?

When you are no longer at the mercy of the clockface and know that you can stretch and bend time to suit your personal needs, answer-ing that question becomes much easier. Those who ask that question, receive the answer, and then take action on that answer lead lives of purpose, meaning, and presence.

The theory of time described in this book, and its practices, have en-abled me not only to know what is mine to do at any moment, but to do it. That's exactly what *All the Time in the World* will help you do as well. Possibly for the first time, we may be ready to not only understand how science accounts for time, but to apply these scientific principles, change our lives, and get on with doing what is ours to do.

Of course, to get to the point where I could reliably "stretch time," as Einstein put it, took a near-death experience, a lifetime of wondering about what causes feelings of timelessness, and decades of practice. Here in these pages, I have distilled all of that down for you into useful prac-tices you can use to focus your perception and change your experience of time. Here's how:

Part 1: Update Your Construct of Time. The first stage is not a practice but a rethinking of the human construct of time. In part 1, I provide a brief overview of the scientific evidence for why time is not the unchanging linear property of human experience we believe it to be.

Instead, based on this evidence, my theory is time is one part physical and one part perception. And because you control the perception part of the formula, you can change your experience of time. This stage is the foundation of our journey, because if you continue to believe time is an unchangeable linear force (despite what science reveals), you won't be successful doing the practices that follow.

Return for a moment to this formula: time is one part physical and one part perception. The physical part of our experience of time is characterized by the world of Einstein, gravity, and relativity where, as a result of Einstein's research and that of many others like him, scientists now understand that time can be stretched, expanded, and contracted like a rubber band. The perception part of time is characterized by the mysterious, fantastic, "spooky" world of quantum theory, where pretty much anything can happen and consciousness causes the collapse of the wave function, a phenomenon that itself may be the source of reality (including time).

This is not science fiction. This is science. This two-part formula is, I believe, a brand-new construct of time that clearly describes a scientifically valid approach for stretching and bending time for ourselves. In science, a theory that combines the classical laws of physics with quantum theory is called a unified theory, or a theory of everything. You might call this theory a theory of everything for time.

Yet as Carl Sagan said, "Extraordinary claims require extraordinary evidence."[1] To that end, the material presented here has been reviewed by mainstream scientists who helped me make it as scientifically rigorous as possible—with the caveat that the issue of what time is and how it works remains one of the biggest unsolved problems in physics today.

Part 2: Master Your Experience of Time. Once you have updated your construct of time, you can begin to focus your perception, change your experience of time, and even affect actual clock time. These abilities may be beyond what is normal or expected, but they are not supernatural or magic—they are still part of our natural human capacities. You'll learn how personal transformation is rooted in time—whether you are conditioned by past experiences, having trouble staying in the present moment, or wanting to manifest the future you desire. As you go through these simple practices, which train you to remain in the state of focused perception where time stretches and bends amidst the busyness of your daily life, you may discover that time is no longer an enemy.

I am not promising that you will never be late to an appointment again or you will never again miss a deadline. However, you may discover that what it means to "be on time" will change. You may also find yourself procrastinating less, thinking more clearly, and behaving more calmly so that you are not only wasting less time but are literally transcending time.

Presented in this book is an idea whose time has finally come. Ancient cultures have presented similar teachings for millennia. As you master the practices in this book, which combine science with personal transformation, you'll build an awareness of time that transcends clockfaces. Liberated from the illusion that time is your enemy, you'll learn to embrace time as an ally so you can have all the time in the world to do what is yours to do.

It's time you knew the truth about time—and how to master it.

2

One Part Physical

Gravity, Motion, and Physical Laws

Time is not only likely to be the biggest issue in your life, it's also one of the biggest issues in science today. Physicists simply do not understand what time is, at least partially, because it does not behave the same way in all circumstances. We do know that time has a physical component that can be measured by scientists. For example, the motion of a clock measures time, and the motion of the Earth propels time forward as twenty-four-hour days and changing seasons. In this sense, the physical component of time may be most simply defined as our experience of moving in and around space. We physically experience time because we experience ourselves and things moving around. This is obviously true when you think about whether it is day or night in different places on Earth. It isn't the same time in New York as it is in Sydney because the Earth is moving.

As a reality on Earth, time is affected by physical laws, most famously by gravity. The motion of nearly everything in the world around us, from earth-bound physical objects to planets, is governed by gravity. Gravity is a byproduct of matter and space. In fact, matter generates gravity. Gravity is why the Earth goes around the sun and the moon goes around the Earth. Gravity is also at least partially responsible for the passage of time.

Time is also relative. Over a hundred years ago, at the age of twenty-six, Einstein published his seminal theory of special relativity.[1] Einstein's genius insight was this: time passes differently for an object in motion relative to an object moving at a different speed, like a stretchable rubber band. Specifically, the faster you move through space, the more slowly time passes for you relative to someone who is moving more slowly. For example, if you go out into space, travel at speeds near the speed of light, and then turn around and come back, from your perspective, you will experience time passing in the same way as always. Yet, when you return to Earth, the clocks on Earth will show a time farther in the future than yours. In a sense, time will have passed more slowly for you relative to those on Earth.

A decade later, Einstein would publish his theory of general relativity to show that the passage of time is also affected by gravity. If you go out into space and find yourself near a strong source of gravity—such as a black hole—you would experience time passing as usual, enter the black hole, and experience the theoretically terrifying effects of doing so. Yet from the perspective of others on Earth, experiencing a weaker gravitational force relative to you, you would appear to greatly slow down and perhaps even appear to stop before reaching the black hole.[2]

Many people have heard that the closer you get to a black hole, the more time is altered relative to clocks not near the black hole. But what they may not realize is that this phenomenon, known as "time dilation," also happens on Earth. Thanks to atomic clocks, researchers have documented that as little as a one-foot difference in elevation on Earth seems to affect the passing of time.[3] In other words, if you put one of these most highly accurate clocks on the top of Mt. Everest and another in Los Angeles, as time passed, the two clocks would each show a different time of day.

In addition to its physical component, time can also be measured by our *perception* of time passing. Often referred to as "subjective time," this aspect of time has also been studied extensively.[4] For example, most adults would say that as they get older, time seems to pass more quickly. Summers last forever when we're children; as adults, years can pass in the blink of an eye. A researcher from Duke University recently theorized that the reason we remember our childhood as lasting much longer than our adult life is due to the fact that our brains process images more slowly as our bodies age.[5] Because the images from our youth were processed more quickly, there are more of them to remember, which has the effect of stretching out the amount of time over which we feel they occurred. In contrast, because our brain's ability to process images degrades over time, we have fewer images to remember from our adult lives, which gives us the sense that we are jumping from one memory to another quickly, as though time has sped up.

What does all that mean about time? It means that time is not what we think.

With that said, we still tend to think of time as progressing forward in a linear, predictable way, without exception. We perceive time passing as we progress through a series of moments, which when experienced, irreversibly become the past. Like an arrow shot forward, we believe that the past is behind us and cannot be changed, and the future is ahead of us and cannot be known for sure. But this belief about time has not always been the case.

In *The Fourth Turning*, William Strauss and Neil Howe offer a very helpful explanation of how our construct of time developed historically. To briefly summarize, humans have viewed time in three distinct ways.[6]

1. *Chaotic.* Initially, before we formed social groups hundreds of thousands of years ago, early humans viewed time as chaotic. Every event was random; there was neither cause nor effect, nor rhyme nor reason.

2. *Cyclical.* Later on, as social groups developed possibly forty thousand years ago and as we began to understand nature a bit better, we viewed time as cyclical. Time progresses in forever-repeating cycles, seen in the movements of the sun (day), moon (month), zodiac (year), and beyond, and reflected in the daily, monthly, and seasonal cycles of human life.

3. *Linear.* The idea of time as a "unidirectional drama" fully took hold by the sixteenth century, when most of the world shifted to the view that time was progressing forward indefinitely, or what the authors call "history as progress."

We should not be surprised to hear that our construct of time has changed over time; it seems natural if we are always learning more about the universe and the reality of time. That also means the more we continue to learn about time, the more likely it is that our construct of time will change again.

Why do we believe so firmly that time is progressing forward indefinitely? In his book *Until the End of Time*, physicist Brian Greene explains how this uniform, one-way direction we currently associate with the progression of time into the future is connected to the second law of thermodynamics and the idea of entropy.[7] The idea of entropy implies that material things always disperse, decline, decay, and grow more disordered—at least the physical objects we can sense. As a result, because we constantly see ice melt, steam disperse, living things grow and age, and things in general change over time from a state of order to disorder, it's easy for us to assume that time always moves forward.

A scientist may think of the laws of thermodynamics as immutable, proven facts about the way the universe works, not subject to doubt or question. But even physicists would say that the laws of thermodynamics exist to generate predictions about how things move around in our material world. These laws describe our physical world extremely well by employing reasonable simplifications of how things work, but they are simplifications and interpretations, nonetheless. Greene uses the example of a steam engine: he points out that while we can generalize about how water molecules will behave when heated up, we cannot, even with the most sophisticated computers today, predict the individual movement of each water molecule as it turns into steam. This is how the science of statistical predictions gained prominence.[8] By looking at large populations of things instead of individual things, outcomes could be fairly well predicted ahead of time. The predictive power of the mathematics of large numbers is also why casinos are reasonably sure they'll make plenty of money even if a couple people win the jackpot, and it's why physical laws, such as entropy, seem immutable and irreversible. After all, Greene asks, have you ever seen a shattered glass put itself back together?

There is one catch, however. Despite this assumption of irreversibility, every major area of science, including the physical science of Newton, the electromagnetism of Maxwell, the relativistic physics of Einstein, and the quantum physics of Bohr and Heisenberg, is based on mathematical equations that do not require time to move forward in order to work. In other words, the scientific equations that govern our world are independent of the direction of time. This suggests these fundamental equations would work just as well if time ran backward as they would if time ran forward.[9] Even physicists maintain it's possible for entropy to decrease on its own, meaning that something could move from disorder to order and put itself back together, even if it's exceptionally unlikely.[10] For me, this calls into question the immutability and irreversibility of entropy and, along with it, the idea that time always moves in a forward direction.

For fun and the sake of argument, here are some theories from modern physics that challenge the inescapable forward march of time.

Wormholes. In 1935, Albert Einstein and Nathan Rosen discovered what would become known as "Einstein-Rosen bridges" and even later become known as "wormholes." Wormholes are distortions in space-time, as described by Einstein's gravity equations, that are like shortcuts in space physically linking distant locations. If you position one of the openings of a wormhole near something whose gravity would bend time, like a black hole, then the two "passageways" would not progress through time at the same rate, conceivably allowing you to travel back into the past or forward to the future.[11]

Quantum uncertainty. At the heart of quantum theory is quantum uncertainty, which states there is a limit to how much we can know for sure about matter on the scale of atoms or subatomic particles. What we can hope for at best is to calculate mathematical chances, or probabilities, of how likely it is that something will be at a particular location or how it will behave. Quantum uncertainty acknowledges the unpredictability of physics, suggesting that pretty much anything can happen at any time if you wait long enough.[12]

Multiverse. Also from quantum theory, the idea of the multiverse supposes that an infinite number of worlds exist and a different path is taken in each of them as choices arise. Because different things may happen in each universe, this theory solves the so-called "grandfather paradox," a classic objection to time travel. The grandfather paradox states that if you were to go back in time and kill your grandfather before your father was born, then you wouldn't exist in the first place to kill him. The multiverse theory solves that paradox in that you could kill a copy of your grandfather in an alternate universe and therefore still have been born in your universe (without addressing the question of how you traveled between universes in the first place).

Quantum entanglement. The quantum process of entanglement says that particles may be entangled with one another and act as though they are connected, even if they are separated by great distances. This would mean that particles could travel fast—faster, in fact, than the speed of light. If particles can travel faster than the speed of light, then they could presumably travel through time, also making time travel possible.

With the exception of wormholes, these theories challenging the forward march of time all rely on a branch of physics called quantum physics. Quantum physics explains the behavior of the smallest-known things, such as atoms and subatomic particles. Because of the tiny, microscopic scale of the world of quantum physics, mathematics is used to predict the behavior of "quanta," which are minute packets of electromagnetic energy. In the quantum world, energy and matter don't follow the same rules as things we can see, feel, and hold. And this leads us to the perception part of time, best explained by the principles of quantum physics.

3

One Part Perception

The Quantum World

Hundreds of years ago, before anyone discovered the quantum world, classical physicists like Galileo and Newton were studying the nature of energy in time and space. They wanted to devise laws that could highly and accurately predict what would happen in the world of things we can see and hold. Later on, about a century ago when equipment became powerful enough, physicists began to study particles not visible to the human eye at the much smaller level of the atom and became "quantum physicists." At the other end of the spectrum, astrophysicists study large bodies in space, like galaxies and even clusters of galaxies, their movement and gravitational fields, and how they affect the other large bodies around them. In a sense, astrophysicists and quantum physicists are both studying particles; one type of particle just happens to be far larger than the other.

So, what *is* a particle? Science uses the term liberally to describe a lot of different things that have mass. But the honest truth is that scientists don't really know what a "particle" is.[1] In the microscopic quantum world, particles are pointlike objects that are fundamental for matter to exist. Unfortunately for scientists, these fundamental pointlike objects that make up matter do not behave the same way as the relatively large things we can sense in our everyday world, including the really large world of planets and suns. For reasons not yet understood, the behavior of these atomic and subatomic particles remains mysterious compared to that of the larger objects of classical physics. For example, these microscopic particles don't seem to follow the rules of cause and effect our daily lives depend on. These particles might be one place one instant and then be found another place an instant later for no apparent reason. In fact, researchers have been able to find no certainty anywhere in the quantum world. In this chapter, I summarize some key principles of quantum physics that affect our understanding of time, but if you want to learn more about the research behind these concepts, see "Appendix A: Additional Science."

The Observer Effect

Here's an example of just how fantastic the quantum world can be. In our visible world, if you shoot a bullet into a pond, it will hit the water. Upon hitting the water, it will generate waves that move away from where the bullet landed in larger and larger concentric circles, which will eventually reach the other side of the pond. If you shoot a different bullet *over* a pond, it will fly through the air and eventually land somewhere on the other side of the pond. In both cases, a bullet moves from one place to another place. But the bullet shot over the pond didn't make the noticeably visible waves that the bullet shot into the water did; instead, it landed on the ground and stayed there. Now, imagine that this scenario applies to subatomic particles like photons (light particles), where a photon is like a bullet, except that it exists as a tiny packet of energy. It sometimes behaves like the bullet you shot into the pond, which created waves, and sometimes behaves like the bullet you shot over the pond, which didn't.

Going back in time before quantum science, scientists believed that light had properties that could only be explained if it were a wave. Over a hundred years later, Albert Einstein proved that certain frequencies of light also existed as "discrete packets of energy," like particles. Soon after that, experiments showed that light could sometimes behave like waves and sometimes like particles. How the photons behaved turned out to depend on whether the scientists observed or measured them. They found it impossible, though, to observe them as waves and particles at the same time.

Something happened when scientists observed the photons that caused them to change. How can particles behave like particles when they are observed and behave like waves when they aren't? Unlike a visible object, such as a bullet, photons seem to exist as enigmas: they can be either particles or waves, depending on whether or not they are observed.

This may be one of the most fantastic conclusions that comes from quantum theory. Photons are photons; they shouldn't magically change from one thing into another. Whether or not a scientist was looking at them shouldn't make any difference. Yet according to these experiments, in the physicists' terminology, observation seemed to cause the "collapse of the wave function" into a particle. And although this debate started with a photon, it is important to note that this is not limited to just photons. Similar experiments, most famously the double-slit experiment (see "Appendix A: Additional Science"), have been done with everything from neutrons to atoms to even larger molecules. *Wave-particle duality*, where observation causes the collapse of the wave into a particle, seems to govern the behavior of the most basic particles of nature. In fact, all fundamental subatomic particles,[2] including the ones that make up matter,[3] exhibit this strange behavior where they can behave like either particles or waves.

As a result, human beings were brought into the quantum mix as a factor in the scientific, measurable physical world. This phenomenon was coined "the observer effect."[4] It has become a principle of quantum physics, which suggests that human observation—in other words, focus—plays a role in assembling reality. While its discovery flew in the face of our experience of the world around us, as well as violated the laws of classical physics, it couldn't be ignored. Almost a century later, it's not just speculation. There is an increasingly reputable body of evidence showing that what happens in the microscopic quantum world is also happening in our everyday, macroscopic world. Some researchers have interpreted the source of the observer effect to be consciousness itself so that the phrase "consciousness causes collapse" has become, in some circles, synonymous with the observer effect. As Max Planck, a founder of quantum theory, said, "I regard consciousness as fundamental.

I regard matter as derivative from consciousness. We cannot get behind consciousness. Everything that we talk about, everything that we regard as existing, postulates consciousness."[5]

Quantum Superposition

If all matter in its tiniest form exists as possibilities until it is observed, scientists theorized that until it is observed, it exists in multiple possible places at once. In 1935, an Austrian physicist named Erwin Schrödinger came up with a way to illustrate this idea using something larger than a photon: a cat. Don't worry, it was a theoretical "thought" experiment—no living cat was harmed in the performance of this experiment. First, imagine putting a live cat in a box, along with a device that could release poison gas if you wanted it to. If the gas was let out, the cat would die. Now, let's say you flip a coin to decide whether the gas is released or not. By using a coin flip, there is a mathematical chance that 50 percent of the time the gas would be let out, the same chance that the coin would land heads or tails. You would then look in on the cat by opening the sealed box, finding the cat either dead or alive.

If the cat were not a cat but instead a quantum particle, then when you opened the box, the act of looking at the cat would change whether the cat was dead or alive. So, in some sense, just as a photon can be both a wave and a particle until it's observed, the cat would be both dead and alive until you opened the box to check on it. Schrödinger's conclusion was, if quantum principles applied to this situation, the cat would be in what has come to be known as a *quantum superposition* of states, meaning the cat would be both alive and dead at the same time. This conclusion bothered scientists a lot because it goes against the rules of cause and effect that are supposed to govern the universe. Typically we would say the poison was let out or it wasn't; the cat is alive or dead in the box, whether we can see it or not. This famous thought experiment is universally used to shed light on the mysterious world of quantum mechanics, illustrating how differently the quantum world behaves from the rules thought to govern the visible world.

Quantum Entanglement

Even stranger, quantum physics also predicts that particles may some-how be instantaneously communicating with one another, even if they're on opposite sides of a room or on other ends of the universe. Particles connected in this way are said to be *entangled*. It works like this. Let's say you and your friend have two very special decks of cards. The reason they are special is that every time you turn over a card, your friend who turns over a card at the same time sees exactly the same card you see. If you turn over the ace of spades at the same instant your friend turns over a card, they also see the ace of spades. Just like your very special card decks, scientists can entangle two photons, then ship one photon to a different location. If one scientist measures some property of the photon, like its polarization, then another scientist in the other location immediately learns the same thing about the other photon. Note that entanglement has been shown for other types of particles besides photons as well. The observer effect is also at work here be-cause those properties of the particles remain unknown until they are observed. Scientists have shown that when two photons are separated by as many as hundreds of miles, whatever happens to one can imme-diately influence the other, almost as if they are able to instantly send signals to one another.

Like so many other aspects of quantum physics, this discovery is a huge problem. If entangled particles are able to instantly send signals to each other, then whatever is being communicated between them would seem to be traveling faster than the speed of light, which according to scientific theory, nothing can do. Undaunted, scientists are working to show that quantum entanglement occurs over greater and greater distances, further challenging our beliefs about the physical world. How particles become entangled, or what causes this "faster-than-the-speed-of-light" correlation, is as yet unexplained. But experiments have proven beyond a shadow of a doubt that *something* is at work to cause this phenomenon. Although Einstein was originally dubious, calling it "spooky action at a distance," it is very real.[6]

The Theory of Everything

At this point, those of us who are not physicists may be asking an obvious question: How can individual particles that are subatomic and microscopic behave so differently than those same particles when bunched in large numbers as visible, macroscopic matter? Quantum mechanics, which governs the world of the microscopic, and general relativity, which governs the world of the macroscopic, are both amazingly well-proven theories. And while both theories sometimes suggest peculiar results that seem to go against accepted reality, when rigorously tested, the results always support the respective theories' conclusions.

Both theories also assert that the same four fundamental forces affect the macroscopic world of objects we can sense as well as the microscopic world of quantum particles. *Gravity* is the force responsible for holding the planets and galaxies in place. The *electromagnetic force* ties electrons to nuclei and binds atoms into molecules. The *strong force* binds atomic nuclei and quarks to one another. And the *weak force* causes the slow disintegration of atomic nuclei. How can the same four forces be at work in what seem to be two completely different worlds?

Scientists have been attempting to develop a theory that explains all four forces in terms of each other, in a way that applies to both the microscopic and the macroscopic worlds. These attempts to develop one single theory that accurately describes the microscopic and the macroscopic is commonly known as the theory of everything, or a unified theory.

Einstein devoted the final thirty years of his life working to connect gravity, clearly at work in the macroscopic world of general relativity, with electromagnetism.[7] Since then, scientists have continued this pursuit, so far linking the three non-gravitational forces.[8] While it is an active area of research, the ultimate scientific accomplishment of merging all four forces has not been achieved. If accomplished, it would have huge implications for those of us interested in changing our experience of time. It would suggest that the laws of quantum mechanics have measurable, noticeable effects on larger, macroscopic bunches of particles in the visible world, even playing a part in assembling matter and changing the reality of time. Recent theories are increasingly connecting gravity to the other three forces in ways that are so ambitious that the phrase "quantum gravity" has become synonymous with the "theory of everything." (For more on the research behind the theory of everything, see "Appendix A: Additional Science.")

Of these scientific theories, two stand out. One is called *string theory*, which works a lot like its name sounds. It suggests that the universe is comprised of two types of tiny vibrating strings, those with two open ends and those that are closed loops. How these strings stretch, connect, vibrate, and divide accounts for all of the matter and phenomena in the universe, including the macroscopic world of general relativity and the microscopic world of quantum theory. Another unified theory called *loop quantum gravity* suggests that the universe consists of networks of "loops" that behave in ways that are quantum, including being subject to quantum uncertainty.[9]

In addition to these theories about how the universe works, researchers are also working toward a theory of everything by trying to demonstrate that the quantum principles governing the microscopic world are also at work in the macroscopic world. For example, researchers are now suggesting that quantum entanglement and wormholes found in space may be the same phenomena.[10] Other researchers performed a thought experiment to show that gravity and quantum mechanics can be reconciled by demonstrating that quantum superposition—remember Schrödinger's cat?—can exist for really large things, like ships in space.[11] And for decades scientists have been working to show that consciousness causes collapse and the observer effect exists for physical things we can sense.[12] Based on the relentless progress of science, quantum experiments on things larger than particles, where quantum theories hold up, seem inevitable.

Let's take a moment to consider the implications of what we've covered so far. If quantum entanglement is real, if matter exists in a state of superposition until it is observed, and if the observer effect assembles reality, literally anything could happen if you waited long enough. When you consider the sum total of thoughts and intentions in people's minds, the possibilities are infinite. An airplane could land in your backyard—which would have nothing to do with the pickle I want to appear on your lap.

And, you could stretch and bend time—which is why my two-part formula for how time works is, in some sense, a theory of everything. The scientific theories that combine gravity with quantum theory into unified theories rely on observation—which I call focused perception—to work. A subatomic particle's state is indeterminate until determined by an outside observer—you. This suggests that reality, including time, is one part physical and one part perception. Because you control the perception part of the formula, you are in control of your perception of time.

So why doesn't "literally anything" happen more often? Well, it might happen more often than we think. Let's say you dropped a glass and saw it fall in such slow motion that you easily caught it before hitting the floor. You'd likely come up with some logical reason explaining how that happened, think it was odd, go on your way, and forget about it. Or you may have said to yourself, *Did I really just see that? That couldn't have happened.* Most of the time, we discount experiences like this. We explain them away. Why? Because they don't fit into our belief about reality. But scientists are increasingly showing these things do happen in the macroscopic world. As Winston Churchill reportedly said about his political adversary Prime Minister Stanley Baldwin, "Occasionally he stumbled over the truth, but he always picked himself up and hurried on as if nothing had happened."[13] The same could be said for all of us when extraordinary experiences happen and we pass them off as nothing.

Another term for this "stumbling over the truth" is what researchers call *selective attention*. Selective attention is when we focus on one event to the exclusion of other events occurring simultaneously. A great example is a clever video with a group of people passing a couple of basketballs to one another.[14] In this video, the players are dressed in either black or white shirts, and the narrator instructs the viewer to count how many times a player wearing white passes the basketball. If you have never seen it before, watch the video before you read further. Spoiler alert: at the end, the viewer is asked whether they saw a gorilla. Sure enough, someone in a gorilla costume walks right into the group of players, turns and beats their chest a few times at the camera, and walks out again. Yet most people (unless they know to look for the gorilla) don't notice the gorilla at all.

This is a perfect example of selective attention: we miss something as big and obvious as someone dressed in a gorilla costume because our focus was elsewhere and we weren't expecting to see it. Because we weren't expecting to see it, the brain tuned it out. Similarly, if we expect everything we see to follow the material laws of physics and if quantum mechanics are also at work in our larger world, then we may be tuning out what is actually occurring. Why doesn't the airplane land in our yard or the pickle land in our lap? Because we get what we expect. Mostly.

Although much of it is still theoretical, the research applying quantum theory to the macroscopic world could suggest that quantum mechanics applies to all of reality—the large, the tiny, and everything in between. Our expectations may not align with the fullness of what science is revealing as possible and true.

The opposite of selective attention is what I am calling *focused perception*, where a person experiences a higher state of awareness characterized by terms such as the zone, flow, and the Now.

In the next chapter, we'll explore further evidence that shows just how large a role human perception may play in our experience of time and our ability to influence or even control it.

4

How the Unseen Creates the Scene

Once we allow that reality may be one part physical and one part perception, we begin to see the gorilla everywhere. For decades, branches of modern science have been studying the premise that unseen forces may be changing the "scene," with compelling implications.

Nonverbal Communication May Alter Electrical Currents

One of the largest bodies of evidence involves experiments using random number generators. In the 1990s, Dean Radin and other researchers associated with Princeton University undertook a project they called the Global Consciousness Project. This research project sought to establish whether large groups of people—as large as the entire planet Earth—might be communicating using nonphysical means. Using a network of computers around the world, each independently running random number generators, results suggested that the behavior of the network of random sources changed during "global events" such as September 11, 2001, when huge numbers of people were likely experiencing shared emotions. Although scientists don't know exactly how and why, the simultaneously felt emotions were correlated to nonrandom number-generating sequences. The probability that the effect was random was calculated to be less than one in a billion.

Over decades of similar experiments, more than 350 separate tests were performed. While the possible effect shown in just one individual event might have been too miniscule to support a correlation, the combined results over so many tests were more significant. According to Radin and others, these otherwise inexplicable correlations could only be attributed to millions of people reacting to cataclysmic events that occurred at the same time as the changes in the otherwise entirely predictable equipment.[1] Criticism of the projects' findings includes questions about what type of event is considered significant, questions about the standards for variations used in the random data during an event, and the fact that the experiments were not blind, meaning that they didn't have a parallel version of events on Earth where the cataclysmic events didn't happen to which to compare the variations in the data. Still, the research has captivated researchers for years, as they wonder whether or not emotions affecting large populations can have a measurable effect. According to science, anything that is measurable is considered "real."

Human Thought May Affect Other Humans' Thoughts, Feelings, and Behaviors

In an article published in 1990 in the *Journal of the American Society for Psychical Research*, the theory of "distant mental influence" suggested that human subjects could influence the rate of destruction, or hemolysis, of blood cells—in particular the subjects' own blood cells in test tubes.[2] This controversial study is part of the field of transpersonal psychology and the associated research on what is commonly called extrasensory perception, or ESP. The researcher who published that study, William Braud, has since released his twenty years of research as a compilation of articles originally published in peer-reviewed journals between 1983 and 2000.[3] Braud's theory of distant mental influence suggests that, under certain conditions, it is possible to know and to influence the thoughts, images, feelings, behaviors, and physiological and physical activities of other persons and living organisms—even when the influencer and the influenced are separated by great distances in space and time, beyond the reach of conventional senses. Because the usual modes of knowing and influence are eliminated in these studies, their findings may indicate unseen modes of human interaction and interconnection beyond those currently recognized in the conventional natural, behavioral, and social sciences.[4]

Human Perception Changes Reality, Including Perceptions of Time

The examples above show evidence that our thoughts and intentions may affect certain forms of physical reality. But can our thoughts and intentions affect time specifically? The answer seems to be yes, and it's quite common.

In sports, we've all heard of athletes shifting into a "zone" where peak performance occurs. In his autobiography, *Second Wind: The Memoirs of an Opinionated Man,* Bill Russell, the legendary professional basketball player who played center for the Boston Celtics from 1956 to 1969, describes a "mystical feeling" that seemed to slow down the game action before his eyes to create something like magic. He says:

> At that special level all sorts of odd things happened ... I'd be putting out the maximum effort, straining, coughing up parts of my lungs as we ran, and yet I never felt the pain. The game would move so quickly that every fake, cut, and pass would be surprising, and yet nothing could surprise me. It was almost as if we were playing in slow motion. During those spells, I could almost sense how the next play would develop and where the next shot would be taken. Even before the other team brought the ball in bounds, I could feel it so keenly that I'd want to shout to my teammates, "It's coming there!"—except that I knew everything would change if I did. My premonitions would be consistently correct, and I always felt then that I not only knew all the Celtics by heart but also all the opposing players, and that they all knew me.[5]

Many other athletes describe it as an almost trancelike state where they become immersed in their thoughts to such an extent that time slows down. The situation before them is now in slow motion: pure experience, with no conscious thoughts.

How are athletes like Bill Russell able to enter this kind of state where time slows down, they perceive what will happen before it happens, and they can perform extraordinary feats? Many theories and much study have been devoted to this phenomenon of time "slowing down" and "speeding up." Have you ever fallen asleep and dreamed for what seems like hours, but when you awaken, you realize you have only been asleep for a minute or two? How about when you are deep in thought or in a project and look up at the clock to realize hours have gone by unnoticed? In his book *Flow: The Psychology of Optimal Experience*, Mihaly Csikszentmihalyi identifies a self-surpassing dimension of human experience that is recognized by people the world over, regardless of culture, gender, race, or nationality. He calls it *flow*, the product of high challenge and the high ability to meet the challenge (see figure below). Its characteristics include deep concentration, highly efficient performance, emotional buoyancy, a heightened sense of mastery, a lack of self-consciousness, and self-transcendence.[6]

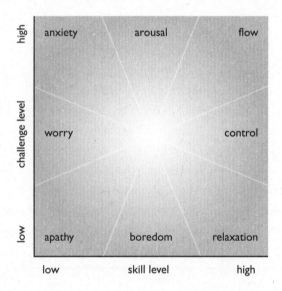

Flow: The product of high challenge and high ability to meet the challenge. Adapted with permission from Mihaly Csikszentmihalyi, *Flow: The Psychology of Optimal Experience* (New York: HarperCollins, 2009).

Others refer to this state of flow as being in the zone, in the present moment, or the Now. It's a state of perception where time doesn't seem to work the way we expect it to. Research shows that being mindful or intently focusing on the present-moment "now" can slow down our brain's perception of time, suggesting that we can slow down our experience of time by intentionally focusing our perception.

Let's take a deeper look at how our perception may change our experience of time. In addition to athletes playing sports, this sense of slowed-down time can also occur for individuals with brain anomalies, especially when their perception of motion is impaired. In one paper, the Zeitraffer phenomenon and akinetopsia were studied in a single patient who had suffered an aneurysm.[7] The Zeitraffer phenomenon is an altered perception of the speed of moving objects, and akinetopsia is the inability to see motion. The patient described one example of seeing water falling out of a shower head stop in the air, each droplet hanging in front of him, like a movie playing in slow motion. Researchers tend to believe that these kinds of experiences exclusively occur when physical diseases are present, such as epilepsy and strokes.

However, as mentioned earlier with the example of my friend Bill in traffic, people facing life-threatening emergencies also experience the slowing of time. Researchers Noyes and Kletti studied this phenomenon over decades, revealing that of the people who had come close to death, more than 70 percent recalled feeling a sense of slowed-down time.[8] Moreover, the speed of subjects' thinking increased to as much as one hundred times the normal rate, events related to the situations they faced were perceived with objectivity and clarity, and because time seemed so expanded, people were able to respond to lightning-fast events with precision and intention.[9]

Researcher David Eagleman, who had a fearful fall through a roof at the age of eight, became so fascinated by what he remembered from his near-death experience that he delved into learning more about it. He performed an experiment with some volunteers who were willing to endure a controlled fearful experience called Suspended Catch Air Device (SCAD) diving.[10] His conclusion was, using a time device worn by each participant, that it isn't the actual experience but the memory of the experience that causes the phenomenon of feeling time slow down. He theorized that when we are in what he called "fear" mode, our brains take in exponentially much more information than normal. We then remember the experience in great detail, suggesting that the feeling of time slowing down was just associated with the way our brain was processing the memory after the fact.

In other research, Sylvie Droit-Volet from Blaise Pascal University and Sandrine Gil from University of Poitiers, France, similarly theorized that when human subjects experience extreme fear, their perception that time slowed down results from changes to our human "internal clock."[11] Subjects were shown clips from three different types of emotion-filled movies and then asked to estimate how long certain events were in duration. After watching the fear-filled movies, subjects perceived events as lasting longer than they actually did. Their conclusion was that fear triggered a "slowing down" of time, while no distortions in perceptions of time occurred after watching the other two types of films. Theorizing about why this may be the case, the researchers explained that slowed-down time experiences were one part physiological and one part perception. The physiology of fear—increased blood pressure, dilated pupils, and fight-or-flight chemicals released into the blood—causes a state of physical arousal that has the effect of speeding up our internal clocks, which slows down time from our external perspective.

These are interesting views, but ones that need some clarification. To me, there is a difference between a feeling of "fear" and a sense of "danger." Personally, I have found that when I feel fear, such as when reacting to a noise in the house late at night, there is no slowing down of time, but when I sense extreme danger, such as when losing control of my car, my perception of time slows down just like it does for athletes in flow, the zone, or the Now.

Research by Daniel C. Dennett and Marcel Kinsbourne may support my view that there is more to our experiences of slowed-down time than merely memories and chemicals. In their paper "Time and the Observer: The Where and When of Consciousness in the Brain," they studied how the eyes, nerves, and brain process what we see in order to try to explain the experience of slowed-down time.[12] They theorized that the brain processes visual information using a feedback loop designed to speed up processing. This feedback loop bypasses the optic nerve and directly instructs the eye—through the retina—what to expect to see. When this happens, such as when a person might be in danger and therefore needs to process a lot of information quickly, the brain might process images out of order. This would cause the person seeing an event to perceive that, for example, time is passing in slow motion. While they conclude that people aren't actually slowing down objective time, it does suggest that the rate at which someone perceives time can change. Moreover, taken to its logical conclusion, it suggests that the rate of passage of time one perceives is somehow subject to what the observer (from quantum theory) is expecting.

I had my own experience of a life-threatening situation not long ago. While driving seventy miles per hour on a highway, a bicycle fell from a truck bed two cars in front of me. As I saw cars around me swerve wildly from side to side, time slowed as I watched the front of my car come upon the bicycle. Then the car seemed to either maneuver around the bike, which was now on the highway, or over it, or through it. To this day I don't know which of those explains what happened. The last thing I remember seeing was the bicycle on the road in my rearview mirror. There was no time to feel fear, but thinking back on it, I was most certainly in danger. In the split second while this was happening, my perception of events shifted into a state of higher awareness that included all of the ingredients that characterize flow, the zone, and the Now: deep concentration, highly efficient performance, emotional buoyancy, a heightened sense of mastery, a lack of self-consciousness, and, afterward, a sense of self-transcendence.[13]

Jim, a police chief, shared a similar story with me. In 1983, Jim was working as a police officer in undercover narcotics at a Southern California police department. On a weekday, around 10:00 a.m., he and his partner were interviewing someone they had arrested earlier in the day. Jim stepped out of the interview room for a minute and learned that there was an armed robbery in progress at a local pizza parlor.

Jim told his partner that he was leaving and drove to the pizza parlor just a few blocks away. When he arrived, three people were robbing the pizza parlor, who Jim discovered had previously engaged in a series of armed robberies and recently shot a highway patrol officer during a traffic stop. They had arrived before the pizza parlor opened, gotten inside, and put all the employees but one into the walk-in cooler. The employee they missed had gotten to a phone and called 911.

As Jim was pulling up to the building, the armed robbers started out the back door of the pizza parlor. Jim could see another officer with his back to the alley that led to the back of the building. Jim found a parked semitrailer where the shadows gave him cover and saw the robbers start shooting at an officer they could see. Two of the robbers went back into the building while one of them ran into a nearby bowling alley, where he was later caught.

Finally, one of the two robbers who had gone back into the pizza parlor came out with a bag of money in one hand and a gun in the other aimed at an officer running toward him. As Jim describes it, from the moment he ran under the semitrailer to take cover, time slowed down. By the time he pulled out his gun and yelled, "Police, stop. Drop the gun. Freeze," time had seemed to come to a complete standstill.

Jim fired his gun three times, and the first thing he noticed was that the sound of the rounds was not at all loud. In fact, he could barely hear the shots as he remembers standing behind himself, looking over his right shoulder at the gun and then at the robber in the distance. As Jim pulled the trigger, he felt the unmistakable sensation of slowness. The gun was a semiautomatic handgun with a slide on top that moves back and forth every time it is fired, with the bullet casing ejected out of the top. Jim remembers seeing the slide moving in slow motion as well as the casings flying out in slow motion. At the same time, he could feel his right arm and shoulder moving back and forth in slow motion with the kick of the firing gun every time he pulled the trigger and the gun discharged.

On the third shot, Jim hit the man in the leg, and he fell down. Jim ran out from under the trailer, and as soon as he did, time returned to normal speed. Afterward, Jim remembered that not only did time and sound slow down for him, even without the ear protectors that are needed to muffle the extremely loud sound of gunfire typically used at the gun range, his ears never rang.

Whether we call it flow, the zone, the Now, or a state of danger, I believe all of these terms describe the same, special state of higher awareness where the classical laws of physics can seem to bend and may even no longer apply. Humans seem to be able to achieve this special state of focused perception remarkably well, but most cannot control it or bring it on at will. The next chapter will explain how, using our brain, we can each achieve this state for ourselves.

5

The Brainwave
State of Focused
Perception

While it makes sense for highly trained professionals and people in grave danger to experience extremely heightened perception and peak focus, can anyone access this special state of focused perception at will? I believe the answer is yes, and the key is our *brainwave state*. Brainwaves indicate the electrical activity of the brain produced by thought and emotion, which travel on the same neural pathways.[1] This electrical activity in the brain is recorded as tracings on paper or computer monitors through the science of *electroencephalography*, or EEG. Brainwaves give us important information about our experiences because EEG recordings represent something that can be scientifically measured. Only recently have we been able to measure brainwaves well enough to see how they correspond to certain levels of focus we can control and change.

To test out whether different brainwave frequencies correspond to different kinds of experiences, I participated in a weeklong session at the Biocybernaut Institute in Sedona, Arizona. There, participants and I completed certain tasks while researchers monitored the different types of brainwaves we generated. Neuroscience tells us there are five different types of commonly studied brainwave frequencies: beta, alpha, theta, delta, and gamma. The brainwaves someone is generating can be measured through special sensors placed on their head. If the feedback is shown to them in real time, the person would have the opportunity to intentionally adjust their thoughts and emotions, which would change the brainwaves being generated. When monitored and displayed using equipment such as they have at the Institute, you can learn how each brainwave frequency plays its own part in the workings of the brain, like I did. Seen in the figure below, the highest frequencies are at the top, and the lower, slower frequencies are at the bottom.

FOCUSED PERCEPTION

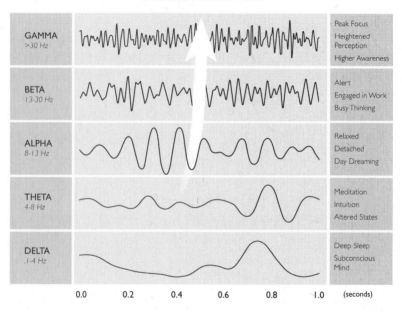

The brainwave frequencies of focused perception

At the Institute, they used light and sound to provide instant feedback when I was generating certain types of brainwaves. I quickly learned that once I could correlate what I was focusing on or feeling to my brainwave pattern, I had a personal benchmark for what brainwaves were being recorded by the brain sensors on my head. For example, intentionally feeling love produced alpha waves. In contrast, thinking intensely busy thoughts by remembering as many things as I could that I needed to do when I got home produced beta waves. This feedback allowed me to reproduce nearly all of the different brainwaves intentionally. Also, after each session, I was able to view the results and look at particular times during the sessions to find out what brainwaves were being recorded while I was doing certain things. I learned that *when I changed my focus, I changed my brainwave state.*

BETA BRAINWAVES:
The Alert Mind

To appreciate the experience of different brainwave frequencies, let's start with beta (from about 13 to 30 Hz), where most people live every day. This is the state of your conscious mind, your reason, your logic, and your active thought processes. It is characterized by alertness, being engaged in your work, and busy thinking. I found that this brainwave state could be "sped up" if I began doing more complex tasks, such as what many refer to as "multitasking."

To practice moving into the beta brainwave state:

1. Begin to think about the list of things you need to do tomorrow or next week.

2. Try to remember all the items on the list once you have made it.

3. Repeat the list to yourself in your mind once you have made it and remembered it.

ALPHA BRAINWAVES:
Relaxed Reflection

In contrast to the alert beta waves, alpha (from about 8 to 13 Hz) indicates someone is awake but resting quietly. Someone who takes a break from work and goes for a walk is likely to move from beta into an alpha state. The experience is often characterized as relaxed, detached, daydreaming, and an optimal state for visualization. I have found that I can move into an alpha state by intentionally relaxing and generating feelings of love and happiness.

To practice moving into the alpha brainwave state:

1. Sit quietly and close your eyes.

2. Begin to reflect on something, someone, or somewhere you love.

3. Picture it in your mind's eye.

4. Put yourself in the picture, holding, touching, or experiencing what you love.

5. Imagine yourself expanding into space as though you are becoming infinitely large.

6. Stay with this thought for as long as you are comfortable, and when you are ready, slowly open your eyes.

THETA BRAINWAVES:
Meditation and Intuition

While at the Institute, after I intentionally moved from beta into alpha, theta brainwaves were also present. Theta waves (from about 4 to 8 Hz) may occur between wakefulness and sleep. They are associated with meditation, intuition, and altered states of consciousness. People who do a lot of monotonous driving may be in theta. Also, runners who are mentally relaxed, experiencing what many refer to as a "runner's high," may be in theta.

To practice moving into the theta brainwave state:

1. Sit comfortably in a quiet place where you can remain undisturbed. Close your eyes.

2. Feel yourself relaxing your body, beginning with the top of your head and working your way down to your feet.

3. Now shift your attention to your breath, to the exclusion of all other thoughts.

4. Continue to focus only on your breath.

5. Notice the repetition of your breath.

6. Imagine what it feels like just before you fall asleep at night, when your eyes are heavy and the world seems very still and dreamy.

7. Remain this way for as long as you are comfortable, and when you are ready, slowly open your eyes.

DELTA BRAINWAVES:
Deep Unconscious Sleep

The brainwave state with the lowest frequency, delta waves (from about 0.1 to 4 Hz), typically occurs during deep, restorative sleep. Delta waves are mostly present during subconscious brain processes. They have been described by some to characterize our subconscious mind as well as our "reptilian" mind, an ancient sensing ability that may alert us to danger before the rational mind is alerted. Most people will likely not experience delta brainwave activity while awake, with the exception of children and those with severe ADHD.[2]

To practice moving into the delta brainwave state:

Go to sleep. Since delta waves are present during REM sleep, when you sleep deeply, you will likely be generating delta waves.

GAMMA BRAINWAVES:
Focused Perception

Finally, gamma waves (greater than about 30 Hz) are the highest measured brainwave frequency and are associated with peak focus, heightened perception, and higher awareness. Believed to be present when someone experiences transcendent experiences, such as *samadhi*,[3] gamma waves may be triggered during states of intense concentration achieved through practices like meditation. Experiments with Tibetan Buddhist monks have shown a correlation between transcendental mental states and gamma waves. One theory is that gamma may be localized in the brain so that the very existence of it indicates an experience of singularity or "unity consciousness."[4] While at the Institute, gamma brainwaves were present in my brainwave measurements during my deepest meditations while I was also completely conscious of what was physically happening around me.

To practice moving into the gamma brainwave state:

1. Sit comfortably in a quiet place where you can remain undisturbed. Close your eyes.

2. Begin to focus on your breath to the exclusion of all other thoughts.

3. Bring to mind someone or something in your life for which you are grateful, such as a life partner, friend, child, or pet.

4. Say to yourself in your mind's voice, "For this, I am grateful."

5. Now see yourself in your mind's eye.

6. Say to yourself in your mind's voice, "For this, I am grateful."

7. Now see your environment or the larger circumstances of your life in your mind's eye.

8. Say to yourself in your mind's voice, "For this, I am grateful."

9. Now begin to generate intense feelings of gratitude from your heart, while focusing on the area of the heart center in your chest.

10. Intensify this feeling by again picturing someone or something in your life that you love.

11. Think of sending the feelings of love up through your body out the top of your head and having them continue to travel upward to infinity.

12. Hold this feeling for as long as you are comfortable, and when you are ready, slowly open your eyes.

The reason this gratitude practice works well is that it brings on a meditative state while you are focusing on your loved ones, yourself, and your life at the same time. Also, it is said that gratitude is the highest form of thought, or cognitive functioning, suggesting that what is most likely to bring on a state of focused perception are the combined states of alertness and meditation—where the mind is highly alert while the body is highly relaxed. This may occur naturally when multiple brainwave states like beta (alertness), alpha (mentally relaxed), theta (meditativeness), and gamma (peak focus) combine into a state of higher awareness, such as that experienced by sports figures playing at the peak of performance, people in life-threatening danger, or people who for whatever reason find themselves in the zone, the flow, the Now, or what I would call a state of focused perception.

Anthony, who also attended the Biocybernaut Institute, described it this way:

> There was a turning point while at Biocybernaut when I realized that the shift from thinking to feeling gets you there. If I had a thought while the sensors were on my head, then I would go into a very contracted and brainwave-suppressed state. But if I allowed myself to feel, particularly to feel expansively, then my brain and my heart seemed to connect in a way where I knew absolutely I was in the moment. And by practicing this shift from thinking, which is beta, to feeling, which is alpha, theta, and gamma, I've been able to change my life so that I exist increasingly in the moment. Because there is no time component to feeling, existing in the moment has become my predominant mode of being.

Using the practices in part 2, you too can learn to intentionally move into this state of focused perception and perhaps even allow it to characterize your life.

How do you begin? By using your brain. (And this doesn't just mean "thinking," as we learned from Anthony.) Each human brain is made up of nerve cells that generate an electric field, the same field which, when detected by certain equipment, is displayed as brainwaves. This field that the brain naturally generates is believed by many to be where thoughts come from. It also determines how each of us experiences our perception of reality. Moreover, because the brain's field is electric (which means it is energy), it is subject to the same scientific theories upon which physics relies. Changes in the energy in the brain's overall electric field result in the different brainwave frequencies.[5]

If we entertain the possibility of a theory of everything where quantum mechanics may also apply to the visible world, then the scientific theories that govern the brain may also include the laws of quantum physics, like quantum entanglement, superposition, the observer effect, and the idea that consciousness causes collapse.[6] Research into new fields, including quantum biology, are increasingly speculating that this might be the case.[7]

This points to the question at the very frontier of science: Just how *is* the human brain involved in the observer effect? What role does the human brain play in the quantum process of observation collapsing the wave function into particles? Maybe waves and particles were always one and the same, and we don't yet have equipment sensitive enough to perceive them as such. Or maybe the observation is some sort of energy transfer resulting from the quantum entanglement between the brain of the observer and what is being observed. Whatever the precise mechanism may one day be discovered to be, in the meantime we do know that we can use our brains to focus on something, which can change our brainwave state, which can change our perception—sometimes for extraordinary results.

Stretching Time

To test out this idea for yourself, let's try a practice to change not only your perception of time, but your experience of actual clock time.

In the 1970s, a Czech scientist named Itzhak Bentov documented an experiment where ordinary people were able to shift into a state of time-lessness or focused perception and see the second hand of an ordinary analog clock slow down or stand still. To try it, perform these steps.

1. Sit comfortably in front of a clock or watch with a second hand closely in front of your face and note the second hand's position.

2. Keep your head still as you look at the clock, and intermittently shift your eyes away from the clock as far to the left or right as you are able. Some people can intentionally blur their vision and take the clockface out of focus, which works also. Do this for a short while, and then use your intention to shift your eyes straight back to fixate directly on the clockface.

3. Try this a few times—blur to focus—so that you can manage this effortlessly.

4. Then, begin to relive a vivid memory that is long and involved, like playing a wonderful movie back in your mind: a place you love, the first time you held your newborn, a memorable kiss.

5. When you look back at the clock, often to people's astonishment, the second hand will appear not to have moved. In some cases, it moves backward. Time has noticeably slowed down during that single second you were lost in thought.

If you are able to slow down or stop the second hand in this practice, it may have been because your mind was focused enough to experience what scientists call *chronostasis*. The medical explanation for this experi-ence is that when you shift your eyes quickly from one brainwave state (reliving a wonderful memory) to another brainwave state (extreme fo-cus), your brain automatically suppresses vision during each extreme shift. The world becomes a blur as the image on your retina is forced to change one way of seeing to another. Then, when the shift is over, your brain replaces the images you lost during the shift with the new image you see in front of you—in this case, the stopped second hand. Our brains may be so good at this that we rarely notice it happening, except when you have an obvious external indicator of time, like a ticking clock. But to your brain, you have just slowed down time.

That medical explanation is accepted among scientists; with that said, I have a different explanation. In terms of brainwave function, closing your eyes and visualizing yourself engaged in your favorite relaxing activity moves you out of ordinary consciousness characterized by a beta brainwave into the more relaxed alpha state. Then, by following the second hand of the clock or watch while noticing the monotonous rhythm of its movement, you are likely to continue and strengthen your state of meditation into one of relaxed, detached, diffused daydreaming while keeping your sensory awareness. After a while, you're likely to also experience a theta brainwave state associated with meditation, intuition, and altered states of consciousness. Continuing to immerse yourself in the feeling of your favorite activity using your senses, while staying awake, moves you into a higher-awareness state of focused perception consisting of the beta, alpha, and theta brainwave states together. Because you are maintaining mental focus, when you slowly open your eyes a tiny bit and gaze softly at the clockface as a disinterested person would, you can easily find yourself in a higher state of awareness where the second hand is not moving or may even be traveling backward. If you reach this higher state, you may be generating gamma waves associated with the zone, flow, the Now—all of which are the same state of focused perception.

In sum, what you've just done is achieve a deeply meditative state, and by watching a second hand on a clock while in that meditative state, you've been able to demonstrate to yourself that this state alters our perception of time.

To create this meditative state in a simpler way, you can begin by sitting quietly and paying attention to the things around you that are pleasant and interesting. Then start actively noticing new things around you. Just this simple practice can enhance your mood and begin to add the alpha and theta frequencies to your brainwave state.

Again, precisely how this works is still unknown, but ample evidence is accumulating that shows the correlation between this higher-awareness brainwave state and the experience of timelessness. As we get better at creating this brainwave state for ourselves, we may one day finally understand the role the quantum world plays in our everyday life and not only validate the theory of everything, but live it. To me, the question is no longer if, but when.

In the meantime, you can learn to move more easily into the state of focused perception conducive for making time stretchable like a rubber band. In part 2, you'll learn practices that will allow you to change your brainwave state, change your perception of time, and become an active part of the unseen that changes the scene.

PART TWO

Master
Your
Experience
of Time

6

Meditation

Create the State
of Focused Perception

When I was in my twenties, I felt I had lost my sense of what was important in life. Not only had I stopped caring about getting things done, I wondered why I was on the planet in the first place. I felt lost and alone. After mentioning this to a friend, he suggested, "Why don't you learn meditation?" I looked into it and ended up choosing the Transcendental Meditation (TM) approach, a very simple way to meditate. Its founder was an Indian physicist who brought meditation to the West and simplified it so that pretty much anyone could learn to do it. TM consists of a twenty-minute meditation practice done twice a day where the meditator repeats a mantra (a Sanskrit word repeated over and over) in their mind's voice.

When I began practicing meditation, the first thing I noticed were the thoughts occurring in my mind, one after another, an incessant voice in my head that would not stop. These thoughts were both about me and the things I should be doing, as well as commentary on what was happening around me. After a while, I worked out ways of silencing that "monkey mind" busy thinking by not attaching to those thoughts and feelings. I found that the more I did not attach to whatever was popping into my head while meditating, the less the busy thinking occurred. Letting go of thoughts and feelings as they occurred created room for deeper things to emerge in my mind, like profound insights, solutions to problems, and genuinely transcendental experiences where I feel like I am part of something bigger than myself.

Today, after practicing meditation for thirty years, I begin with a mantra meditation and soon slip into a state of having no thoughts and no feelings, a state of being deeply quiet. When I do notice a thought or feeling occurring in my mind, or something physically going on around me, I simply make a mental note of it and return to the state of quietude in my mind—a meditative state.

What is a meditative state? In one sense, it is being completely present. It is a mental state achieved by being conscious or aware of the present moment, something most people find very difficult to do. We tend to get stuck in the pain of the past, our worries about the future, or the fantasies we create to escape our present. Learning to return to the present moment, to what is happening Now, is the first step not just to mastering time, but to mastering yourself. It is the state we have been calling focused perception.

In this state, you can observe your thoughts and feelings without judgment, allowing them to simply exist and pass through your awareness, without needing them to be "bad" or "good." This act of nonjudgmental observation helps bring thoughts under greater control, which results in calmness, clarity, and concentration. Meditation also brings on brainwave states conducive for changing our experience of time.

The scientific benefits of meditation are well-documented: reduced worry and stress, increased memory, greater focus, less emotional reactivity, and greater self-insight, morality, and intuition. Also, certain brainwaves become more prominent, including theta and delta. In these brainwave states, we're more likely to have inspirational flashes of creativity, recall forgotten memories, and experience lucid dreaming. Research has also shown that meditation reduces the busy thinking "monkey mind" part of the brain that causes mind-wandering and thoughts about one's self.[1] Physical benefits have also been documented: a recent study found that long-term meditators (who had been practicing for twenty years or more) showed less age-related brain deterioration than non-meditators.

Further, meditation appears to result in increased volume of key areas of the brain that govern learning, memory, and the regulation of emotions, and decreased volume of areas responsible for fear, anxiety, and stress.[2]

However, despite the known benefits, the scientific explanation for *why* these many benefits occur is not at all settled. Many of the benefits of meditation have to do with how our brain works, how thoughts arise, and where they come from. This highlights the issue of consciousness, also known in science as the "hard problem of consciousness."[3] Consciousness is a "hard problem" because of a seemingly unreconcilable gap between the physical world, which includes our physical brain processes, and the nonphysical world, which includes our mind, thoughts, and feelings. For example, Where do thoughts come from? Why do we have experiences that "feel like" something? This nonphysical world of mind, thoughts, and feelings is what we think of as consciousness. Some scientists believe they already understand where consciousness comes from and how it works, while others believe we have not even scratched the surface of the answer. As a result, researchers are increasingly turning to the mysteries of quantum physics to explain the mystery of consciousness. With the discovery of the observer effect over a hundred years ago, evidence of consciousness has already seemed to impose itself onto quantum theory. Some scientists concluded that consciousness must be included as a viable factor in quantum theory. Others, including Einstein, did not, with Einstein famously remarking, "I like to think the moon is there even if I am not looking at it."

In stark contrast to Einstein, Nobel Prize–winning physicist Roger Penrose proposes that not only does consciousness influence quantum mechanics,[4] it exists because of it. Penrose suggests that there are molecular structures in the human brain that alter their state as a response to a quantum event—just like particles do in response to the observer effect.[5] While challenged by the scientific community, Penrose remains unfazed. Moreover, since Penrose's research, others have discovered evidence of quantum effects in living beings, such as migrating birds using quantum mechanics for navigation.[6] So while there seems to be no conclusive evidence that quantum theory can explain consciousness, it remains hard to believe that a purely physical definition of consciousness can account for proven phenomena like the observer effect. Consciousness may not entirely create our reality—by "reality" I mean what is measurable—but if reality is one part physical and one part perception, consciousness may certainly play a role in affecting the chances of possible outcomes occurring in our everyday, macroscopic world.

How does this discussion about consciousness and the observer effect relate to meditation? Here's a real-life example. One day I was sharing the science behind the observer effect and "consciousness causes collapse" with Anna. She understood the concepts but still felt a large chasm between what she understood about the quantum world and her own lived experience. She wasn't sure she could make the leap from her normal daily experience of conscious thoughts to a deeper experience of herself and how the world works, according to quantum principles.

To experience the difference, I suggested she begin with the meditation technique I share in the next practice. I told her this was the simplest way I knew to drop into a state of focused perception, otherwise known as the zone, flow, or the Now. The very next week, she told me she was amazed by the results. "I feel like my entire sense of self has expanded," she told me. "I hadn't realized I had been living as if my thoughts and feelings were all there were to me. But with the practice you gave me, I noticed there was a part of myself that could watch my thoughts and feelings and that was bigger than my thoughts and feelings. I could experience a part of myself that was connected to the divine and always at peace."

What she was calling "connected to the divine" may be the same as whatever the observer effect might be for humans. This experience has been described as feelings of oneness, unity, peace, and transcendence, what I am calling the state of focused perception. Just as Anna described, when you are able to notice your thoughts and feelings occurring while not attaching to them, your experience of yourself expands. You may realize that you are more than your thoughts and feelings. And you may experience yourself as an observer watching your thoughts and feelings, perhaps the same observer physics has identified.

Here's a simple meditation practice that makes the most of the science you've already learned. Through this practice, you'll not only experience the present moment, which is crucial to mastering time, but you'll also enjoy greater concentration while awake, better memory and learning ability, less fear and anxiety, and reduced brain activity related to self-referential "me" thoughts. Most importantly, you will be generating the brainwave state of focused perception, which is key to changing your experience of time and the foundation of all the practices that follow.

PRACTICE: CREATE A STATE OF FOCUSED PERCEPTION[7]

Practice this one in darkness, whether it's by closing your eyes, turning off the lights, or wearing an eye mask. Sit comfortably on the floor with your legs folded in front of you (commonly called the lotus position) and rest your hands on your lap with your palms up. If this posture is uncomfortable, sit on a small pillow with your legs folded in front of you, or sit against a wall with your legs stretched out in front of you.

Notice your mind working: Is it reflecting on something that happened in the past? Is it planning for something to happen in the future? Is it noticing something around you? Simply allow the thoughts to occur as they come to you, and then turn your focus to your breath.

Begin to inhale through your nose and exhale through your mouth, with your exhaled breath twice as long as your inhaled breath. Imagine your exhalation as smoke or mist leaving your mouth.

With your next exhale, see the numeral 3 appear before your closed eyes. With your next exhale, see the numeral 3 change to the numeral 2. With your next exhale, see the numeral 2 change to the numeral 1. And with your next exhale, see the numeral 1 change to the numeral 0.

Remain in this state of quiet, focused perception for as long as you want. When you feel ready, slowly open your eyes, or continue with another practice.

Advanced Technique:
Puppies and Kittens

Inevitably conscious thoughts will arise. To release them easily, use a practice I call "Puppies and Kittens." When any thought comes to mind, turn it into something you love, like a puppy or a kitten. Focus on the thought, and then intentionally take that puppy or kitten and put them "outside." This will have the effect of removing them from your awareness. If they return, just put them outside again, until they no longer return. Here's the hack: you can't fight thoughts when you meditate. With this practice, you can allow them to happen, yet not attach to them.

Advanced Technique:
What Is Mine to Do Today?

Although this practice is the foundation of all those that follow, it can also be a standalone practice to access deeper wisdom and clarity. In the state of focused perception, you are fully in the present, free from regrets of the past and fear of the future. You are in a state where you are observing your thoughts and feelings without judgment. You can take advantage of this state of greater calmness, clarity, and concentration by asking yourself a question you'd like to know the answer to, such as, *What is mine to do today?* When you have received the clarity or sense of completion you need, slowly open your eyes.

7

Imagination

Experience Your Life in Advance

Years ago, I moved from New York City to Florida. I had an outdoor shower on my terrace in New York and wanted the same at my new home in Florida. I packed the shower myself, taking special care to pack the part that connected the shower to a hose, a unique five-inch plastic tube with a socket on one end, which I believed was virtually irreplaceable without buying an entirely new shower. When I arrived in Florida and began to unpack, it was extremely hot outside. I decided it was time to use my wonderful outdoor shower. I went to my back porch, where the shower was still in its box. I opened the box and looked for the part, which I had carefully taped to the shower using duct tape. It wasn't there.

Exasperated, I dumped out the box and began going through all of the contents, which included other things that had been on my terrace in New York City. The part was nowhere to be found. I finally gave up, locked up the house to leave, and went out to my car. When I opened the door of the car, I looked inside before jumping into the seat. To my astonishment, the part for the shower was lying on the gas pedal.

My car had been shipped by truck and arrived a few days earlier. I had driven it every day since it arrived, and I never before saw the five-inch plastic tube with its vibrant orange socket, the missing part for the shower, until that moment. How did it get there? Did my thoughts somehow make it appear? Was I imagining the whole episode? I'll never know. What I do know is that I took the part back upstairs, installed it, and got my shower running.

As children, many of us believe that we can use our thoughts, or our imagination, to influence not just our inner world, but our outer, physical world as well. Often called "magical thinking," the science of this experience is well studied. Researcher Jean Piaget theorized that magical thinking is central to a child's cognitive development. It results from egocentrism, the belief that someone is the center of the universe, combined with limited reasoning ability. As the child matures, this imaginal thought is eventually replaced with rational thought compatible with widely agreed-upon scientific principles, like cause and effect.[1] For some people, however, magical thinking can continue into adulthood, in spite of their exposure to scientific reasoning. Piaget uses the example of religious beliefs that grow out of socialization or cultural conditioning, typically addressing issues such as the meaning of life, what it means to exist, and what happens when we die.

Many scientists maintain that magical thinking experienced by adults—such as believing we can use our imagination to affect the physical world—may be evidence of brain abnormalities, with schizophrenia being an obvious example. But recent studies in brain science reveal that as many as 27 percent of people are missing a characteristic of "normal" brains that allows them to distinguish between what is being imagined and what may be really happening. Researchers found the results surprising because the experimental subjects were otherwise healthy, educated adults who reported no history of mental disorders.[2]

While these scientists view the belief that imagination affects reality as a brain disorder, others have found that imagination plays an important role in creating our physical reality. As just one well-cited example, researchers at the University of Chicago discovered that "mental practice," commonly known as "visualization," was nearly as effective as physical practice for groups of high school basketball players practicing free throws.[3]

Studies like these suggest that our imagination—in the form of mental practice, or visualization—can be used to enhance our performance in sports and other physical activities. Yet perhaps the largest body of evidence that our perception affects physical reality is hidden in plain sight: the placebo effect. Long considered to be a liability in clinical trials, the placebo effect refers to the reliable percentage of people who experience positive effects from a fake treatment when told the treatment is real. Recently, researchers have begun to view the placebo effect through a positive lens; for example, Harvard Medical School's Program in Placebo Studies and Therapeutic Encounter studies all aspects of the placebo effect, including the mind-body connection, the patient-provider relationship, the medical ritual, the provision of care, and the meaning of the treatment to the patient, in order to help improve patient outcomes.[4]

Imagination certainly plays an important role in our lives; at the very least it generates intuition, stimulates new ideas, and results in insights and innovations. As Einstein once said, "The true sign of intelligence is not knowledge but imagination." If imagination is our ability to form new ideas, concepts, and images of external objects not present to our senses, it influences everything we think about, create, and do. It has resulted in theories and inventions crucial to expanding everything from science to the arts.

But with the discovery of the observer effect and the idea that "consciousness causes collapse," imagination may play an even larger role in quantum mechanics than it does in our macroscopic physical world (much to the discomfort of scientists then and now). In fact, the worldwide race to build the first quantum computer points to the belief in science that such a computer would be capable of performing tasks that far exceed our ordinary computers—by mimicking the human brain. While ordinary computers calculate using billions of physical switches that are either on or off in the form of transistors, quantum computers calculate using atoms and subatomic particles. Because these particles may be either on or off at the same time, at least until they're measured, quantum computers can run simultaneous calculations. As a result, there have already been reports of quantum computers operating at millions of times the speed of state-of-the-art supercomputers.

Might whatever the observer effect is be assembling reality in our larger world through our imagination? A few years ago, I really needed a friend to repay a loan I had made to them. I knew their circumstances were such that repaying me sooner rather than later was a problem for them, and they also felt badly about it. So instead of focusing on the negative, I instead imagined the moment when everything had worked out for them to repay me, and they were so happy they were hugging me while handing me the check. In this way, everyone would benefit from something I really wanted to happen, and it wouldn't be a detriment to anyone. Eventually, that scene happened almost exactly as I had imagined—and although I had not been repaid as soon as I would have liked, the outcome benefitted us both.

Now, it's your turn. Try this practice in which you use your imagination to experience something you want to have happen in advance. By starting with the "Create a State of Focused Perception" practice from chapter 6, you will be stimulating a brainwave state that includes theta waves, which are related to intuition and altered states of consciousness. By using your imagination as a tool, you may be able to create more of the life you want instead of simply wishing for it—perhaps saving yourself the time it would take to create that aspect of your life through your physical effort alone.

PRACTICE: EXPERIENCE YOUR LIFE IN ADVANCE

Begin by relaxing your body as deeply as you can using the "Create a State of Focused Perception" practice in chapter 6.

Think of something you would really like to create for yourself. I recommend choosing something that benefits everyone involved and doesn't harm or detract from anyone or anything. After decades of using these practices, I've learned that when I devote a little extra effort to thinking about how everyone and everything can benefit from something I want to have happen, instead of just thinking about how it benefits myself, the outcomes I want seem to more reliably happen.

Imagine that what you want to create has already occurred in every sense: visually, experientially, and emotionally. Put out of your mind any explanation for how it has happened; simply accept that it is done and complete. Immerse yourself deeply in the sensations of what has been created as well as the feeling of relief or satisfaction that it is already accomplished.

When you are ready, slowly open your eyes.

Note: If you're having trouble feeling that what you want has already occurred, imagine you are diving into the feeling like it's a giant lake. See yourself bathing in it, so you feel immersed in the sensations like water.

Advanced Technique: Dream Your Life Three Years in Advance

If you aren't sure what you want to create, you can use a similar practice called "Dream Your Life Three Years in Advance."[5]

Begin by relaxing your body as deeply as you can using the "Create a State of Focused Perception" practice in chapter 6.

Imagine seeing yourself from afar, seated exactly as you are right now. Now, imagine a bubble surrounds you and lifts you up from wherever you are seated so that you are now seeing your home, office building, or other current location below you.

Imagine the bubble beginning to move to your right as you see the Earth move to your left below you. Continue to imagine the bubble moving until you sense you have moved three years into the future. See the bubble stop and lower you back down to Earth. Notice your surroundings. Where are you? What are you doing? Who are you with? Do not feel you must create what you are experiencing; simply notice it. By imagining yourself three years in the future, you can get a sense of what you want to create for yourself and your life.

Once you have made note of your life three years in advance, imagine the bubble again surrounding you and lifting you up. See the Earth move underneath you as you imagine the bubble now moving to your left. When you sense you are two years in advance—meaning you have gone back in time one year from where you just were—imagine the bubble putting you down. You are in your life as you imagine it two years from now. What do you see?

See the bubble surround you again and lift you up. See the Earth move underneath you as you imagine the bubble again moving to your left, this time traveling to the time one year in the future. Imagine the bubble lowering you down to Earth once more. What do you see now?

Finally, travel back to the present time so that you're sitting exactly where you are right now. Write down what you saw, including any insights about the path it may take to get there.

8

Trauma

Reverse the Past

Entering the state of focused perception is the basic skill you need to change your experience of time at will. However, research shows that we almost universally avoid focusing on the present in favor of reliving the past or worrying about the future.[1] Becoming stuck in an endless loop of regrets from the past and fear of the future can keep us from the state of focused perception and therefore from mastering time.

Not to worry. If you find that your thoughts about the past or future keep getting in the way of the present, so that the state of focused perception feels elusive, the practices in this chapter and the next will help relieve painful thoughts of the past and worry about the future, removing the obstacles to a state of focused perception and allowing you to change your experience of time.

For some, the pain of the past is their primary obstacle to fully experiencing the present. When Margaret was a little girl, her mother was very involved in the church and left her alone repeatedly in the church building as she did her volunteer work. Margaret recalls that when she was about five or six, while being left alone, she was molested by the janitor. Margaret told her mother, but instead of rallying to Margaret's defense, her mother blamed her. This extreme childhood trauma—the memory of the molestation and the perceived betrayal by her mother—set Margaret off on a debilitating course in life. Even today, decades later, she has episodes of such poor self-esteem that sometimes she can barely work. She interprets many if not all of her daily experiences as being part of the same past trauma. This constant reliving of the past effectively freezes Margaret in time, so that she is unable to move beyond the event and go on with her life.

Derived from the Greek word for "wound," trauma is defined as an event that causes a severe mental, emotional, and/or physical response. The range of events that could be considered traumatic include sexual assault, like Margaret experienced; however, any event in someone's life could be experienced as traumatic, whether it's a threat to their own life or another person's life, an incident questioning one's moral integrity, or an encounter with violence and death.

Years ago, Danny experienced a trauma where his emotional response was regret. When Danny was away at college, he kept in touch with a good friend from his hometown. He looked her up when he came home for breaks between semesters and often spent time with her. His friend graduated before he did, became successful in her career, and often returned to their hometown on weekends so the two of them could stay in touch. One evening when she was in town, they had a couple of drinks and went back to Danny's house. She needed to drive home because she had an early business meeting the next morning. Danny encouraged her to stay the night, to not drive home after she had been drinking, but she refused. Danny chose not to insist, since he wasn't her boyfriend and he had always thought of her as older and wiser. His friend got in her car and left. That night she lost control of her car and died in a horrific accident. Danny blamed himself for her death, regretting that he did not insist that she not drive herself home. Like Margaret, the event had the effect of freezing Danny in time as he continued to relive the tragedy in his mind.

In both of these cases, a trauma occurred that forever altered the course of their lives and resulted in negative emotions. In one case, the person directly experienced a traumatic event; in the other, a tragic event occurred that resulted in a person inflicting trauma on themselves in the form of self-blame.

Trauma and regret are the result of viewing the present through the lens of the past. That's not always bad; context is important. But when we continually look at the present through the lens of the past, the present becomes the manifestation of the past—and keeps us from fully entering the present as it is.

For example, while experiences of trauma can result in healthy, normal emotions like anger, anxiety, fear, and sadness that fade over time as healing occurs, sometimes these emotions can slow down and even prevent healing. In Margaret's case, the fear resulting from her trauma could have had the positive, protective result of causing her to be careful in choosing her friends, and her outrage could have resulted in standing up for herself as an adult, but they did not. And while Danny's guilt about his actions that night could have resulted in apologizing to his friend's family and working on himself to restore a positive self-image, it did not. In both cases, those emotions resulted in no corrective behavior. To the contrary, both people developed self-images so altered by trauma that their feelings of worthlessness, helplessness, inferiority, and being fundamentally flawed kept them trapped in time. They both felt paralyzed, unable to do anything to alleviate their feelings. These feelings can be so deeply felt that they not only dominate someone's private thoughts, but negatively impact personal relationships to the point where someone can feel dangerously disconnected from the world.

Fortunately, the science around trauma has advanced so that researchers understand it better, particularly its resulting impact on the brain. For example, scientists long believed that the brain was similar to the physical body: once maturity occurs, the brain stops growing or developing. If the brain was injured or subject to disease, the possibility for recovery would be very limited. But recently, researcher Norman Doidge has suggested that the brain is constantly changing itself in response to experiences and events.[2] This branch of research called *neuroplasticity* suggests that the brain is able to perform extensive self-healing—not just from trauma, but from debilitating diseases like autism, stroke, and Parkinson's.

For Margaret and Danny, this research would suggest that the effects of trauma and persistent regret are temporary and will fade in intensity as the brain rewires itself. But that didn't happen in their cases. In fact, critics of neuroplasticity point out that this same rewiring feature of the brain can result in stubborn, self-destructive habits that don't serve people going forward. Or the brain may adapt in such a way that the psychological defense against future trauma is more self-destructive than the trauma itself.

Other critics suggest that Doidge's discovery of neuroplasticity is irrelevant, having no effect one way or another on someone's psychological development.[3]

Another field of study may be more promising for healing trauma at the level of the brain and freeing people from being psychologically stuck in the past: mindfulness.[4] In the state of mindfulness, you can observe your thoughts without judging whether they are bad or good. Another benefit is that mindfulness can stimulate thoughts of being in control, which results in feelings of calmness, clarity, and concentration. From the perspective of time, mindfulness means that someone is conscious or aware of the present moment. This means that trauma, which is rooted in the past, cannot coexist with a brain that is in a state of mindfulness, which is the here and now. Mindfulness elicits the brainwave states including alpha, theta, and gamma, which may be present during experiences of higher awareness. As you may have already guessed, meditation is the practice that elicits the state of mindfulness, which is also how we move into a state of focused perception. Here is the challenge we face: the pain of the past can interfere with experiencing mindfulness, and yet mindfulness is precisely what we need to relieve the pain of the past.

Is there any way we can break the cycle and influence the literal past? From the perspective of quantum theory, at the level of quantum particles, the answer is yes.

Devised from the concept of wave-particle duality, where observation determines whether light will behave as either a photon or a wave (and where until that observation, it could have been either one), a thought experiment originally performed by physicist John Wheeler in the 1970s reveals that actions taken in the present do influence what happened in the past. Called "delayed-choice quantum-eraser" experiments,[5] they work like this. These experiments begin with the classic "double-slit experiment" originally used to prove wave-particle duality. Imagine there is a source of light, as pictured on the next page. The photons shoot out of it, pass through the two slits, and appear on the screen on the other side. If the photons pass through both slits, researchers observing the experiment would see an "interference pattern" of bright and dark patches, which are the result of light acting like waves.

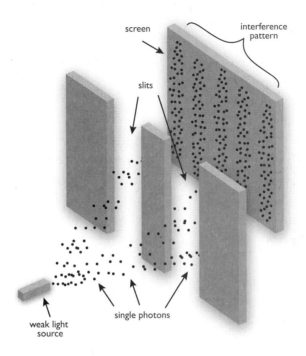

Double-slit experiment

Now, here's where the thought experiment begins. Imagine that the screen on the other side of the slits is not there. The photons being shot out of the light source would keep going like bullets shot out of a gun, never being detected by any screen that would determine whether they ended up as waves or particles. But what if the choice to have the screen or not have the screen is decided *after* the photons pass through the slits? If we consistently apply quantum principles, the result is that light changes itself from a wave (with the screen) to a particle (a photon) after the moment in time that determined whether or not there was a screen had already occurred—as if it traveled back in time and changed itself from a wave into a particle.

In 2007, researchers in France again performed the double-slit experiment by allowing a single photon to pass through the two slits.[6] They then used a random number generator to decide whether or not the screen would be on the other side to detect it, as well as equipment that could switch from screen to no screen faster than the photon could travel to the screen if it were there. Even when the experiment was extended to shoot the photon from Earth to space—over twenty-two hundred miles—the results were the same: the photon's past was not set in stone; it could change depending on what happened in the present.[7]

Photons live in the quantum world and behave very differently from the macroscopic world around us. With that said, there is something mysterious and fantastic about a scientific outcome that suggests what happens in the present can change the past. A way to put this quantum principle in practice is to use an ancient technique called *reversing the past*, which combines the skills of focused perception and imagination. In it, you use your imagination to go back to a trauma you have experienced, relive the events surrounding it, and change how it ends.[8] Danny used it to successfully move past the blame he placed on himself for his friend's death by reliving that tragic decision in his mind and then changing what happened next. Although it didn't immediately release him from those traumatic thoughts of the past, by repeating the practice daily for twenty-one days, he was able to resolve the guilt he felt while becoming more at peace with the reality of someone's physical death.

Reversing the past can be used with any past experience that creates negative feelings in the present; it doesn't have to be traumatic. In fact, I reverse my day every evening (see the advanced technique below), seeing any negative outcome of the day reversed into the best possible outcome, to erase any influence my negative feelings about today's events may have on the future.

Of course, reversing the past can't erase your actual experience of the event (or can it?). But what is certain is that you can change your feelings about it, freeing yourself from the past, enabling yourself to enjoy the present, and possibly assembling a brighter future for yourself.

PRACTICE:
REVERSE THE PAST

Relax as deeply as you can, using the "Create a State of Focused Perception" practice from chapter 6. When you see the numeral 0 appear before your closed eyes, shift your focus to some experience in your life that you want to change and rid yourself of. It could be a minor experience or something significant. If you sense there's a deeper trauma behind a minor event but aren't sure what it is, start with the minor event.

Begin to relive the sensations of where you were and who you were with. Bring up any emotions related to the experience, like anger, fear, resentment, frustration, sadness, or anxiety. Welcome the negative emotions. Hold the experience and the emotions in your mind as though all of them were happening again to you right now, in the moment.

Now, reverse whatever you felt was negative about the experience so that instead it is fully resolved. Allow all issues and questions surrounding the experience to dissolve from your thoughts. Breathe a sigh of relief and feel fully empowered by the sense that the issue is resolved.

When you are ready, slowly open your eyes.

Advanced Technique: Reverse an Experience in Real Time

You can use this practice to reverse any negative experience that happens throughout your day. For example, when I have a conversation with someone I feel badly or angry about, I immediately find a quiet place to close my eyes, practice focused perception, relive the conversation up to the point where something unpleasant was said and then change what was said so that when the reimagined conversation ends, I feel good or peaceful about it.

Advanced Technique: Reverse Your Day

You can also use this practice to reverse the events that happen to you at the end of each day. As you lie in bed just before you fall asleep, think of the moment you first opened your eyes that morning. Then go through your day changing each experience into the best possible version of what could have happened for you. Continue to do that for all experiences you remember from your day until you have completely relived your day and you find yourself once again in your bed, ready to fall asleep.

Advanced Technique:
Reverse a Dream

Reversing the past also works on dreams. If you wake up disturbed from a bad dream, you can use the practice above and in place of a past event, relive the dream in great detail up to the moment it becomes disturbing. Then see reversed whatever was negative so the best possible version of your dream happens before your eyes. Complete the remainder of the practice as written above.

Advanced Technique:
Reverse Past Trauma

If you are experiencing persistent negative emotions related to a particular scenario, you aren't sure why, *and* you are ready and willing to work on the deeper cause of your negative emotions, you can begin with the practice "Receive Insight When You Need It" (see chapter 11). When you have a sense of what the source of your negative emotions might be, you can reverse it using the practice above. When you get to the part where you see your situation resolved, imagine that your wisest, kindest adult self is now present with you in the event. What was most needed in this moment to resolve or heal all these negative emotions? See your adult self providing whatever is needed for you. Feel all the positive emotions that occur now that the event is fully resolved in the best possible way. Complete the remainder of the practice as written above.

9

Worry

Don't Let the Future
Slow You Down

Fear of the future can also be an obstacle to achieving a state of focused perception. For example, I live in a remote place, so I regularly use a house alarm at night. One night I had a feeling that even though I set the alarm before bed, I was somehow not alone. Living with me are animals who would have sensed the presence of another human being in the house, and they were sleeping peacefully on the bed with me. Still, I felt paralyzed by thoughts I could not stop. This sense of fear gripped me so much that I did not sleep much of the night. Because the alarm was set and the animals were not agitated, my fear was completely irrational. At the time, I did not sense slowed-down time, which I've often experienced when in danger. That tells me I was not in a state of focused perception during this experience; something else was going on.

Fear, and the less intense version of it, worry, are not like other feelings. As I experienced that night, fear affected every aspect of my body and thoughts. It reduced my rational ability to make sense of events around me, and it paralyzed my physical body so that at times I couldn't move. As we know from brain science, different brainwave states are generated by thoughts and feelings. A recent study examined what occurs in the brain when people were exposed to fearful images.[1] What was novel about this study is it attempted to separate people's thoughts from the innate human and animal response to fear, or fight-or-flight. It also paid special attention to how our brain prioritizes what it perceives as threatening information.

Participants in the study were randomly shown images that were either not recognizable due to visual distortions or clearly recognizable. The images were either pleasant and nonthreatening or unpleasant and threatening. While wearing sensors on their head, people pressed buttons to record what type of image they had just seen. As expected, the fearful images immediately resulted in higher beta brainwave activity, associated with innate responses of fight-or-flight. But the researchers also uncovered that the unpleasant, fearful images resulted in increased theta brainwaves, usually associated with creativity, inspiration, and insight. The theta waves began in the part of the brain where the brain's amygdala fear center is located, then moved to the hippocampus where the brain's memory center is located, and finally moved to the frontal lobe, where human intelligence and imagination are believed to be located. The researchers used the term "move" to describe the general direction of electrical signals given off by neurons in the brain. In other words, it seems fear "moves" throughout our brain, affecting not just our conscious thoughts and feelings, but our memories, ideas, and imagination.

While it was a small study, it did shed light on how to possibly treat persistent episodes of fear as well as what triggers sudden flashbacks to fearful events. And while worry may be felt less intensely than fear, it still begins with a thought in the brain that results in certain brainwaves being generated and moving from one area to another as the thought takes hold.

What this means to me is that fear and worry can be neutralized by the brainwave state of focused perception. Specifically, the focused perception that results from meditation is shown to reduce fear and worry as well as eliminate self-referential thoughts associated with beta brainwaves, like *What will happen to me?* And from a physics perspective, the observer effect explains how quantum particles behave depends on whether scientists are focusing on them. Either way, focusing your thoughts can have measurable effect on how you experience the present.

The night I was so gripped by fear, I eventually got a hold of myself and used the practice below to stop the uncontrollable fight-or-flight thoughts. I knew from my work at the Biocybernaut Institute that if I began to relax deeply using focused perception, I could change my brainwave state from a fear state to a relaxed and reflective alpha brainwave state, and then to a meditative theta brainwave state. I employed the steps below to first intensify the feelings of fear and then to suddenly stop those feelings by focusing on the fact that I was fine and completely safe in the moment. The relief I felt likely resulted in mentally relaxed theta brainwaves, associated with focused perception and the experience of transcending time.

If you're finding that fear or worry about the future is getting in the way of being conscious of the present moment, then your experience of time is being affected, just as it is when you're focused on the past. Stuck in the worries of the future, you are literally squandering time in a way that no amount of stopped clocks will ever help you experience a sense of ease and flow. The next time a worrisome thought occurs, or you are gripped by a sense of fear, try the practice below. Instead of being paralyzed, you can instantly change the perception part of the one part physical and one part perception equation, and shift your brainwave state to one conducive for higher awareness. Not only will you become better able to access the state that allows you to transcend time, you'll keep yourself from wasting time worrying over the future so that you can do something about it in the present.

PRACTICE: DON'T LET THE FUTURE SLOW YOU DOWN

Relax as deeply as you can using the "Create a State of Focused Perception" practice in chapter 6. When you see the numeral 0 appear in front of your closed eyes, shift your focus to the fearful or worrisome thought that you want to neutralize and rid yourself of.

Begin to fully experience the emotion of fear by imagining in detail the unpleasant circumstances that would result in you or others being harmed. If you're experiencing a minor worry, intensify the worrisome thought to the extreme experience of all the unpleasant things that could happen. Intensify the emotion of fear until you feel the sensations in your body. Hold the experience and the emotions in your mind as though all of them were happening to you right now, in the moment.

Now stop, and instead become aware that the experience never happened. Right now, in the moment, you are fine, there is no unpleasantness, you are completely safe. Say to yourself, *Oh, that's not what happened at all*, or *It didn't happen that way*. Allow all thoughts and sensations you imagined might happen to dissolve from your mind. You don't know how or why, but just dive into the feeling of relief that the unpleasantness never happened in the way you imagined. Your mind may object, so just set that objection aside. If an objection comes up again, that's okay. Just continue to set those thoughts aside.

Feel fully free from the unpleasantness, which could include a sense of safety or a positive outcome. See yourself breathing a sigh of relief that the unpleasantness never happened. When you are ready, slowly open your eyes.

Advanced Technique: What's True?

To neutralize persistent recurring fears, you can use a practice adapted from author Charles Eisenstein.[2] It works best with a partner. For example, if you're experiencing fear about losing your job, begin with the "Create a State of Focused Perception" practice. Then open your eyes and write down the bare facts of the situation and at least two different interpretations of those facts. Have your partner begin by asking you, "So, you think you're going to lose your job. What's true?" You respond with what's true by reading the two different interpretations. Then your partner asks you again, "What's true?" and you again respond with two different interpretations of the facts.

Continue this back-and-forth until you begin to see the way your brain may have been distorting the facts of the situation to result in unpleasant interpretations of what might happen. Eventually, you will uncover what is really true, which is likely not to be as unpleasant as you feared.

10

Focus

Stretch Time

A couple of years ago, I was visiting friends on the Upper East Side in New York City. I was leaving the apartment where I was staying to meet my friend at 11:00 a.m., who was waiting for me at a café all the way across town through Central Park. It was 10:50. If you know this part of New York, you're probably already thinking there was no way I was going to make it on time. Not only was my destination too far away to reach in just ten minutes, but my taxi ended up behind a fire truck, slowly backing into a fire station, in the middle of a one-way street.

As I was riding in the cab, I dropped into a meditative state and focused my perception. Instead of allowing myself to feel anxious, I stared at the old-fashioned clockface on the dashboard while visualizing myself getting out of the car when the minute hand struck 11:00. That's exactly what happened: I stepped out of the cab at 11:00 a.m. and was on time to meet my friend.

How could I have arrived at my destination on time? In chapter 3, I mentioned the theory of loop quantum gravity. The physicist behind that theory would say that our perception of time doesn't even correspond to physical reality. In *The Order of Time*, physicist Carlo Rovelli points out that even Einstein characterized time as a stretchable rubber band that shortens and lengthens depending on one's speed or proximity to mass compared to another's—and how scientists keep ignoring that fact.

Instead, Rovelli believes that reality and further theorizes that time is actually an intricate collection of discrete particle-like things onto which we, through our perception, project the past, present, and future[1]—like an infinite number of four-dimensional blocks representing all of the events that could ever happen at any time and at any place.[2]

Loop quantum gravity is the theory I like best to describe time. I have long had the sense that the real universe occurs in individual instants on a moment-to-moment basis. For me, whatever the observer effect may be for humans plays a part in assembling reality: events before they happen exist as potentialities in multiple locations at once, and particles are entangled by an unknown force—similar to Rovelli's discrete space and time particles. This means that, like loop quantum gravity theory, pretty much anything can happen, something that has been my personal experience. It also means that we live in a world without limitations.

Perhaps you have already been stretching time without realizing it. We've read some accounts of how people experience a slowing of time during moments of extreme danger. But nearly everyone I've interviewed has had their own personal, less urgent stories of experiences where time didn't pass normally because affecting time *meant something important to them*. They may have needed to make a plane flight so they could be at the bedside of a loved one before they passed. Miraculously, everything falls into place, and they were where they wanted to be for an important moment. I experienced this myself when I needed to fly across the country on a moment's notice to be with my mother before she died; I made it with time to spare. For me, these are instances of the observer part of our perception stretching time so that we can take care of what is meaningful to us.

Just recently, Amanda shared her experience of stretching time with me. She regularly drives her sons to sailing practice after school down a busy highway undergoing road construction with many traffic lights. In her experience, it can easily take twenty to twenty-five minutes to get to the dock.

"The funny thing is," she said, "it seems that no matter what time I leave, I always get there on time—give or take one or two minutes.

Before the road construction began, it would take ten minutes to get to practice, so often I will forget and leave ten minutes before practice begins. Yet even with the road construction, I arrive on time. And even when I leave twenty or twenty-five minutes ahead, I still get there at around the same time.

"I'm usually not worried about being late," she continued. "I'm not sure why, but I just believe we're going to make it on time, like it's a fact."

Amanda also told me that this hasn't always been her experience. "Back when I drove the kids to preschool, I was really worried about being late. I believed the teachers would see me as a bad mom if I was late, which made me even more worried about being late, and truthfully, I often *was* late. It felt like a self-perpetuating cycle."

"What's different about driving them to sailing practice?" I asked.

"Well, when I was driving them to preschool, I was focused on myself and was afraid of being judged, which I think created this self-perpetuating cycle of fear," she said. "But with sailing practice, I'm not thinking of myself at all. I'm only thinking of them, and how much they love sailing and their teammates, and what a great experience they will have. It's all positive. Strangely, I'm not worried about being late, and somehow I almost never am, even when it seems I should be."

Amanda was describing the difference between a beta brainwave state, associated with fight-or-flight, and a state of focused perception, where the observer may be in the driver's seat. Time could stretch and bend as needed when she was focused on what was most important to her, without anxiety.

If this is how time works, then what if we could just slow it down for ourselves when we need to? And if so, how? The key is our brainwave state. When we feel anxious about being somewhere on time, our state of fear (as opposed to danger) brings on the chattering, monkey mind of beta brainwaves. By resisting that trap and returning ourselves to a meditative state of focused perception, which includes alpha and theta brainwaves, we may be able to achieve extraordinary results with any clock, any time.

PRACTICE:
STRETCH TIME

In chapter 5, you may have tried Dr. Bentov's experiment of stopping the second hand of a clock by changing your brainwave state. You can apply this same technique to any clock that governs whether or not you will be late. For example, if you are stuck in traffic and have a clock on your dashboard, focus on the clock (note that digital clocks do not have nearly the same effect as the motion of second hands, but will do in a pinch).

Note: This works best if you are not driving. If you are driving, see the advanced technique below.

First, gaze softly at the clock as a disinterested person would. Notice the monotonous rhythm of its movement or of the numbers changing. Use your intention to shift your eyes straight back to fixate directly on the clockface. Repeatedly shift your eyes away from the clock to the road, or wherever else you are, and then back on the clockface.

Begin to imagine a vivid scene of arriving at your destination on time, like playing a movie of it in your head. Continue playing this movie of arriving on time for as long as you are traveling to your destination, intermittently shifting your eyes away from the clock to the road or your surroundings.

Advanced Technique:
Be on Time (When Driving)

If you are driving and you must get somewhere on time, keep your eyes on the road and think about the positive benefits to you or others if you arrive on time. Feel your positive desire to be on time, in order to benefit all parties involved. Then, let the desire go. Create a movie in your mind of arriving to your destination on time, seeing all the positive outcomes of doing so. Remind yourself that you have all the time in the world to get to where you need to go. Imagine time stretching and shifting around you to make room for however long your journey needs to take. Continue to replay that movie of arriving on time in your mind until you reach your destination.

11

Thoughts

Receive Insight
When You Need It

Most people credit the theory of evolution to Charles Darwin around 1840. But did you know that the same theory was developed independently by Alfred Russel Wallace?[1] The instances of inventors and scientists coming up with the same idea independently of one another are countless. In the eighteenth century, oxygen was discovered by both Carl Wilhelm Scheele and Joseph Priestly around 1774.[2] In the nineteenth century, the first law of thermodynamics was theorized by Germain Hess, Julius Robert von Mayer, and James Joule, among others.[3] And the big bang theory of the universe, suggesting that the universe is expanding away from an initial location, was developed independently by both Alexander Friedman and Georges Lemaître.[4] You just need spend a little time researching "multiple discoveries" to see how many major breakthroughs occurred at different moments in time around the world with no connection whatsoever. Are these truly coincidences? Or do we possess some sort of collective memory we can access?

The phenomenon of multiple independent discoveries exists as a body of scientific research, investigating how living things learn and transfer that learning to each other and subsequent generations without directly interacting. In a 1920 experiment, a researcher at Harvard University put rats through experiments for twenty-two generations using a water maze. He observed that rats related to other rats that had already experienced the maze, even those identified as slow to learn, found the solution almost ten times faster than first-time rats whose relatives had not experienced the maze. This experiment was later recreated in Scotland and also Australia.[5] This research suggests that biological systems, from ant trails to the coordinated movement of schools of fish, may be self-organizing, which means they have the ability to arrange themselves spontaneously in a nonrandom way without the help of an external organizer. While this field of study still faces a lot of open questions about how these complex systems result from the synchronized behavior of millions of participants, some theories do exist.[6] In addition to general physics explanations like reductionism and emergence,[7] Rupert Sheldrake's theory of "morphic resonance" suggests self-organizing systems result from a collective memory possessed by each participant in the system to which it contributes. According to his research, when a behavior is repeated often enough, it forms what he calls a "morphogenetic field" that generates a "morphic resonance" through space and time.[8] Systems believed by Sheldrake to have this ability include molecules, crystals, cells, plants, animals, and animal societies. Although condemned by critics as heresy, Sheldrake's views are not that easily dismissed. Trained as a scientist first at Cambridge and then through a Royal Society fellowship, Sheldrake bases his theory on the idea that memory is somehow inherent in nature—a phenomenon that continues to show up in other branches of science.

For example, the fields of biology and quantum science are coming together to explain how biological systems that exhibit synchronized behavior, like migrating birds, may be subject to quantum principles.[9] Other researchers are investigating how quantum processes, like entanglement and superposition, may be governing behavior found in nature.[10] And quantum mechanics is increasingly being suspected of being present in the human brain's processes as well.[11] If so, then innumerable billions of disparate patterns could exist all at the same time. Then, perhaps assembled by whatever the observer effect may be for humans, the single pattern that emerges is what occurs to the person as a conscious thought.[12]

This theory would suggest that the size of a physical brain would not necessarily determine the quality of thought or even whether or not one is thinking. Sheldrake also theorized that the human brain may be processing fields that do not rely on the physical brain, perhaps by acting as a sort of antenna. Supporting this theory are accounts of humans either born with as little as 25 percent of a normal brain or who undergo surgery to remove parts of their brain. In many of these cases, people lived normal lives with average IQs even though they possessed very little in terms of a brain[13]—suggesting once again that consciousness may be quantum and therefore nonlocal, meaning that thoughts might exist somewhere outside in the physical world and not just in biology-based organisms.

If our brains generate energy patterns from a quantum field and act as antennae for a field of thoughts that surround us, we may be able to think pretty much any thought at any time. I used this approach to writing the material found in this book. As I began to explore the many possible explanations for the unusual experiences of my life, I followed threads of research deep within fields I had no formal training in but instead imagined I was already familiar with, including physics, quantum physics, biology, and brain science. Answers to my open questions seemed to spontaneously come to me at times I never expected. In some sense, this book explores ideas in science that were not yet explored by me, a nonscientist. Of course, I also completed my due diligence: the material contained in this book has been reviewed and deemed scientifically rigorous by a mainstream scientist.

When we enter the state of focused perception, we generate theta brainwaves (among others), which are often associated with the hippocampus, the part of the brain associated with memory. Perhaps this state also increases our ability to access collective memory. When you feel like you're stuck or wasting time, and need insight quickly, try this simple but powerful practice.[14] I use it whenever I feel paralyzed by some thought or feeling that prevents me from being completely present or taking an action that I want to take. I know that those paralyzing thoughts and feelings are not only affecting how I experience time, they are resulting in squandered time. And until I return to a state of focused perception, time is not my ally but my enemy.

PRACTICE: RECEIVE INSIGHT WHEN YOU NEED IT

Sit comfortably where you can be undisturbed and under no time pressure. It's best if you're alone, although you don't need to be. It's also best if your eyes are closed and even better if you're in darkness. None of this is necessary; it simply optimizes your brain for receptivity.

Bring yourself into a meditative state using the "Create a State of Focused Perception" practice from chapter 6. Then, ask yourself this question: *What do I myself know about this?* Insert the subject you want to know about at the end of the question, such as, *What do I myself know about why I keep putting off calling my brother (or making the doctor's appointment, or asking for a raise)?*

Sit quietly for as long as you want. Don't worry about not immediately getting an answer, although you will always get an answer of some kind that pops into your head. When a thought, idea, image, or answer comes to you, remember what it is, such as, *I'm afraid my brother will criticize me.*

Repeat the question, this time inserting the answer at the end of the same question: *What do I myself know about why I'm afraid my brother will criticize me?* Wait for the new thought or answer, and again insert that thought or answer at the end of the same question.

Repeat this sequence of questions and answers until you feel you have more information than you did when you started.

12

Telepathy

Reach Others Fast

In a recent experiment conducted by researchers from Harvard Medical School, Axilum Robotics (France), and the research firm Starlab (Barcelona), an individual in India was able to communicate the words "hola" and "ciao" to three other people in France using only brain-to-brain communication. "Brain-to-brain communication" means that the words were spoken, texted, or typed nowhere, but only occurred in the brains of individuals participating in a research study. This was one of the first proven instances of brain-to-brain communication known to exist, and researchers hope it will inspire further research and one day provide new forms of communication for those unable to speak.[1] Does this mean telepathy is real? Numerous research initiatives suggest it is.[2]

One such experiment performed at the University of Washington involved sending a brain signal from one researcher to the other side of the campus, causing another one of the researchers' fingers to move on a keyboard.[3] Described as the "first human brain-to-brain interface," researchers hooked themselves up to an electroencephalography machine, which records electrical activity in the brain. They put on caps with electrodes, with one of the researchers' caps placed directly over the part of his brain that controls hand movement. While the two cross-campus labs were working in coordination, there was no communication between them. Then, one of the researchers played an imaginary video game where he imagined moving his right hand to hit the space bar to "fire" a cannon (without actually moving his hand). At the same time, across campus, the other researcher's right index finger moved involuntarily. Although this experiment was one-way communication, researchers are looking at ways to demonstrate two-way conversations directly between two brains.

Brain-to-brain communication doesn't seem to be limited to human beings. In the 1960s, Cleve Backster was considered to be at the forefront of the art of interrogation when he created the CIA's first polygraph unit. The method used in polygraphs (i.e., lie-detector tests) is galvanic skin response, which refers to changes in the electrical resistance of someone's skin as a result of their emotional stress, measured with a tool called a galvanometer. Later in Backster's career, his interest shifted from testing humans to testing plants and animals, which began almost by accident when he decided to hook up his house plant to lie-detector equipment. He discovered that plants and other biological life may be able to detect and respond to human thoughts and emotions without any physical contact between the two, through the process of galvanic skin response. This research was later expanded on in the 1973 book *The Secret Life of Plants* by Peter Tompkins and Christopher Bird.[4]

A quantum explanation for these phenomena may once again be found in the intersection of quantum mechanics and biology. As I explained in part 1, although no one has ever witnessed quantum processes in our macroscopic world, scientists are increasingly wondering just how far-reaching the effects of the quantum world might be and whether they extend far enough to clearly influence living things. Recently, researchers reported the successful entanglement of biological matter (in the form of bacteria) with particles of energy (in the form of photons), providing more evidence that quantum theory's transition from the theoretical to the physical may not be a question of if, but when.[5] Still, other research is attempting to show quantum entanglement for a macroscopic particle that is not in a brain but in an inanimate object. The most classic example is the Bell test from the 1960s, which for decades has been cited as confirmation that quantum entanglement occurs in physical things.[6] Recently, researchers decided to rerun the Bell test using one hundred human volunteers. The volunteers, wearing headsets that read brain activity, were instructed to affect the outcomes of random number generators located one hundred kilometers away. The results aren't yet conclusive, but if they ever are, they may go a long way toward demonstrating that particles exhibit meaningful quantum behaviors in the macroscopic world.[7] Either way, the possibility highlights just how unconventionally quantum theory compels us to think about how our world works.

From a brain-science perspective, researchers believe that our brains may be hardwired to pick up on the intentions and emotions of others when they are in our presence.[8] But to connect across any amount of distance, whatever that wiring may be has to allow one person to tune in to the same "frequency" as another person. Researchers believe that the brain's limbic system may be part of this wiring.[9] The limbic system deals with memory as well as emotions by regulating chemicals released as a result of emotional stimuli. A brainwave frequency identified with the limbic system is theta, which makes sense as theta brainwaves are associated with intuition and altered states of consciousness.

I frequently send thoughts to others during my workday. Recently, I needed to ask a friend, an expert in accounting, a time-sensitive financial question. Instead of immediately calling him, though, I relaxed at my desk using focused perception. I then visualized my friend Rich, who lives in New York, as though he were right in front of me. I focused on sending the words, "Call me," as though I were speaking directly to him. I have found that sending a simple word or image works best. I called him just as the deadline expired—and he answered on the first ring. After I said, "Hello," he said, "I was just thinking of calling you." I've even taken turns sending and receiving messages with a friend who knows I am sending them messages, but they don't know what those messages say. Try it on others as well as pets; you might be surprised to discover how strong a mental connection you and your friends have.

PRACTICE:
REACH OTHERS FAST

Begin by quieting yourself and entering a meditative state using the "Create a State of Focused Perception" practice in chapter 6.

Bring to mind a vivid scene of what you want to experience as a result of sending your message, such as answering your phone and hearing the voice of the person you've been trying to reach, or looking at your email inbox and seeing the email you've been waiting for unopened.

Visualize the person you want to receive your message. If you are far away from the receiver, it might be helpful to look at a picture of them before you begin visualizing them.

Call to mind the feelings you experience when you interact with the person face-to-face. Feel these emotions as if the person were actually in your presence. Focus on these feelings and believe that you are creating a connection with the other person.

Focus on a single image or word you want to hear or read. Visualize it with as much detail as possible and focus your mind solely on it. Concentrate on what it looks like, what it's like to touch it, and/or how it makes you feel.

After forming a clear mental image, transmit your message to the person by imagining the words or object traveling from your mind into the receiver's. Visualize yourself face-to-face with the receiver, and say to them, "Cat," or whatever thought you're transmitting. In your mind's eye, see the look of realization on their face as they understand what you're telling them.

Now become aware that what you want to happen has already occurred, completely, in every possible way. Feel the sense of relief that there is nothing more to do. What you wanted to have done is already fully done. Let that sensation wash over your body, like diving into a giant lake, deeper and deeper.

When finished, abruptly stop and open your eyes. By doing so, you will drop out of the meditative state and stop thinking about the vivid scene, as your brainwaves shift to beta.

13

Supersight

Instantly Verify
What Matters Most

While living in Florida, I was evacuated as a result of multiple hurricanes. One in particular was forecasted to directly impact my community, and my house was in a critical flood zone. We were issued a mandatory evacuation, and I did not have enough time to pack up all my belongings. While evacuated, I used the tool of my imagination to "see" everything safe and dry (see chapter 7). I did not watch the horrifying pictures on the news; I instead simply focused on the image of the house being undamaged. I also used remote viewing to check in on my house, to "see" if the interior was unaffected. When it was safe to return, against all odds, I walked into a dry, undamaged house. While neighboring homes flooded, for some reason mine did not. The only apparent damage was as a result of the ocean flooding the yard all the way to the outer wall of the house but not entering it. Whether it had merely comforted me to "see" the house intact or whether there was more to it, experiences like mine are neither unusual nor new.

Most people have had experiences like seeing a sudden image of a friend in need or somehow knowing a chance encounter would happen moments in advance. In fact, humans have reported these kinds of experiences, often referred to as second sight, extrasensory visions, or remote viewing, for thousands of years. Remote viewing occurs when humans are able to view objects and locations they are physically separated from and which would be otherwise be impossible to see. According to researchers at Stanford Research Institute (SRI), remote viewing is very real.

In the mid-1970s, the Central Intelligence Agency was reported to have hired SRI researcher Russell Targ to help develop the capability of remotely viewing targets, such as people and places.[1] Over about a decade, a stable of remote viewers was nurtured to determine whether they could remotely view people and locations of national interest.[2] In one case, remote viewer Keith "Blue" Harary was asked to report to SRI during the Iran hostage crisis. While there, he seemed to identify a hostage, Richard Queen, held by Iranian militants. Queen was desperately ill with multiple sclerosis, which Harary saw while remotely viewing. After the Iranians later released Queen, apparently because they did not want him to die in their custody, an American medical team confirmed what Harary reported about Queen's poor health. Later on, when Queen was debriefed, he is reported to have become irate at the thought that one of his Iranian captors must have been working for the Americans, because how else could the United States have known about his condition?[3]

Can we access information beyond our sensory awareness? That question remains un-definitively answered, although nonparanormal disciplines, like physics, may explain it. When Einstein colorfully called the quantum physics phenomenon known as entanglement "spooky action at a distance," he was referring to particles that seem to instantaneously influence one another, as though entangled, even when far apart. This idea of "nonlocal consciousness" suggests that the human mind can somehow operate outside the classical laws of physics and may also be subject to the laws of quantum physics. Although "spooky action at a distance" was dismissed by Einstein during his life, physicists have now verifiably observed objects being influenced by nonlocal forces that are greater and greater distances apart. How far apart can entangled particles get? No one knows, with recent demonstrations being as distant as from Earth to a satellite in space.[4] Could the hundreds of thousands of remote viewing experiments observed by scientists be evidence of quantum entanglement?

Out of this intriguing thought was born the field of study called quantum consciousness, which considers whether phenomena like remote viewing, receiving thoughts (chapter 11), and sending thoughts (chapter 12) can be explained by quantum theory. As more research is conducted, we may discover that experiences we think of as transcendent do exist and can be explained by science.

Pulling together everything we've learned so far, here is a possible explanation for how remote viewing may work. If quantum entanglement is possible, some aspect of your subconscious mind may already know information about what you want to see remotely (the target). Information coming from your subconscious mind may be able to be interpreted by your conscious mind. By practicing focused perception and generating theta brainwaves, which are associated with intuition and altered states of consciousness, you may be creating a way to communicate that knowledge to your conscious mind. Generally, though, it doesn't happen anything like getting a clear picture in front of your eyes. Instead, people report that remote viewing occurs through subtle sensations and feelings, which they then interpret.

By the way, you don't have to be a spy to use remote viewing in positive and productive ways. My friend Carly uses this approach to help others find lost pets. And I use it regularly when I need to find lost keys or glasses. Of course, any tool can be used inappropriately, just as it can be used for good. That said, many people now believe that anyone can achieve striking results with remote viewing. Try this practice and see for yourself.

PRACTICE: INSTANTLY VERIFY WHAT MATTERS MOST

In preparation for this practice, ask an assistant or friend to choose five to seven pictures to cut out from a magazine or download from the internet. These need to be pictures of real-world places that are iconic and known to you, like the Eiffel Tower, the Grand Canyon, or a big city. These will be your "targets." Ask them to place the pictures facedown in a stack in a sealed box or envelope.

When you're ready to begin, have blank paper and a pen or pencil next to you to write down your impressions. Then relax your body as deeply as you can using the "Create a State of Focused Perception" practice.

Begin to imagine how it would feel to be someplace else in your home or environment, such as outside if you are indoors or in the bedroom if you are in your living room. The more relaxed you are, the more intently you will be able to focus on the feeling of being in another place.

Now imagine you are inside the box or envelope of pictures, looking down at the stack. Turn over the first picture with your mind. Take in just basic impressions of what you are seeing. Try to notice what you feel is the most imposing image in the target: Is it natural or constructed? Is it on land or in the water? Write down the first thing you see.

Draw a sketch of the target. Really take the time to observe the colors and shapes of what you see.

Now imagine you are floating over the target several feet above it. Note on your paper your impressions about the target from above.

Complete this practice with the first target by writing a brief summary of everything you saw. Write down any information that comes to you in as much detail as possible while not judging anything. Be sure to include sensory information, like a smell, colors, a taste, or the temperature. You might see blurry shapes and patterns. These are called "dimensionals." Note if you feel an emotional reaction to the target.

Remove the first photo from the stack and compare it to your impressions.

When ready, repeat these steps for each picture in the stack.

Once you are finished, if you didn't connect with anything in the photo, don't be disappointed. One of the objectives of remote viewing is to learn things about yourself as well as the target. Remote viewing is an ability you may be able to cultivate over time with great success, so you can apply it to what matters most to you.

14

Love

Harness
Metaphysical
Gravity

One evening, a woman and her husband were waiting at a traffic light in their pickup, on their way home after having dinner. A Camaro abruptly pulled out in front of them, and to their horror, they saw the Camaro hit a cyclist and continue driving. After about thirty feet, the speeding car stopped with the cyclist still underneath. The husband got out of the truck and lifted the front end of the Camaro off the cyclist just enough to allow its driver to pull the badly injured cyclist free. Although an experienced weightlifter, the husband to this day cannot explain how he did that, saying, "There's no way I could lift that car right now." The world record for deadlifting a weight is about eleven hundred pounds, and the Camaro weighed three thousand pounds. The man somehow instantly summoned the ability to lift what was likely about fifteen hundred pounds of the total three-thousand-pound car off a total stranger to save his life.[1] In this moment of extreme danger, he spontaneously exhibited incredible strength to perform this heroic feat. Researchers refer to these episodes as "hysterical" or "superhuman" and suggest that the body's release of adrenaline in the face of life-threatening circumstances can contribute to them. But according to biomechanical research, adrenaline isn't enough to turn an otherwise average human being into Superman.[2]

Another theory is that when we are doing something for someone else, such as the man who felt an urgent need to save the cyclist's life, we may be able to transcend the fear and physical discomfort that would ordinarily preclude us from performing such heroic acts. In 2014, marathoner Meb Keflezighi won the Boston Marathon. He ascribed his surprising win to his intense desire to honor the victims of a terrorist attack that happened just a year earlier at the same marathon.[3] In fact, a study of hundreds of thousands of workers across a diverse range of industries found that when participants' jobs positively affected others, both their motivation and job performance improved, resulting in feelings of self-transcendence.[4] The focused perception of these people and others who experience this sense of self-transcendence would likely show up as meditative brainwave states such as theta or gamma. For marathoner Meb Keflezighi, his intense desire to honor others meant he literally ran faster than all others in the race. For others who feel their jobs positively affected others, it meant less time wasted and more efficient performance. But is that all there is to it?

A notable figure in science believed there was more. The twentieth-century futurist Richard Buckminster Fuller suggested, "Love is metaphysical gravity."[5] This belief was apparently formed during his search for the principles governing the universe. For him to succeed in identifying these fundamental principles would require the laws of physics and nature to be based on one universal process—a theory of everything. To Fuller, the continuous energy flowing through our brains as ideas, feeling, dreams, and emotions bears a striking resemblance to electromagnetism. And love bears a striking resemblance to gravity as the assembling force of the universe.

A new theory supports Fuller's idea, suggesting that whatever generates the thoughts, feelings, and desires in our brains—consciousness—is based on quantum theory. Called quantum cognition, this theory combines neuroscience with psychology to suggest that consciousness is not a computer, but instead a sort of quantum-based universe. And being quantum based, this universe allows for the ambiguities and paradoxes that are routine in quantum mechanics, including wave-particle duality and quantum superposition.[6] The effect is that we can hold competing ideas, feelings, and emotions in our brains until, under some quantum process, they are resolved just like Schrödinger's cat. That's one half of Fuller's theory. The other half, "love is gravity," is one which even physicists note bears a striking similarity to entangled, subatomic particles. Love is mysterious and links people together in ways we don't understand. And love is a lot like quantum entanglement, where particles can be intimately linked to one another, even when great distances are between them. Recently, researchers have studied whether entanglement might be the link between gravity and the quantum world.[7]

Not that any of this proves that love is actually quantum gravity. With that said, many people have experienced unexplainable events involving people we care about,[8] including me. A friend for whom I felt a lot of affection needed to refinance his home in Manhattan right after the Great Recession of 2008. He had an urgent need to reduce his loan payments, and the interest rate he was locked into was far greater than current rates of interest as a result of the stock market crash. Every day, I imagined the same thing for my friend: sitting with him at a conference table handing him my Montblanc pen to sign his new mortgage. While also doing what I could to try to find a lender who would take on his multimillion-dollar mortgage, I imagined this scene every day for one year while also desiring it for him from my heart. Then, in 2010, as a result of a chance meeting of an old acquaintance, I happened upon a lender who was willing to do the loan when all others had declined. In April 2011, I sat at the conference table I had imagined and handed my friend the pen. The lender then remarked, "How did this loan happen?" I looked across the table at the lender and said, "Beats me," while turning to smile at my friend. I knew my intense desire to help another had a hand in an extraordinary outcome that would otherwise have taken much longer or never happened at all. In some sense, my strong affection changed my friend's timeline.

There are many books on what people call "manifesting." But I have discovered that the most powerful way to "manifest" reality is to desire something for someone else out of true affection or love. Why is it the most powerful? Because desiring something for someone else generates feelings and not thoughts. When we intensely desire something for someone else, thoughts that can turn into fear are unlikely to arise. We're not afraid that person won't get what they want; it doesn't have much, if anything, to do with us. That's why desire for another, from affection or love, contributes so powerfully to creating things we want to happen—whether desiring something as small as your kids being on time for sailing practice, or as large as a multimillion-dollar mortgage. This experience is a state of focused perception, where self-transcendence takes over and brainwaves like theta, delta, and gamma are present. If love might be present in the laws of the universe, then when you feel intense love, you may generate a brainwave state of self-transcendence that actually affects your physical world, if reality is indeed one part physical and one part perception.

To create from a state of affection or love, you can use the practice "Experience Your Life in Advance" (see chapter 7), seeing every experience you want to happen that day in a movie starring you. As with any movie in your mind, the key is not to dwell on it; see it, and let it go immediately. Why? If you dwell on it, your brain will begin to generate fearful thoughts and undo the state of focused perception your feelings may be creating.

Or you can try this practice, "Harness the Metaphysical Gravity."[9] It's been practiced in the major spiritual cultures around the world for hundreds and thousands of years, such as Judaism (Kabbalah), Christianity (by mystics such as St. Teresa of Avila), ancient Egypt, and India.

PRACTICE: HARNESS METAPHYSICAL GRAVITY

Relax as deeply as you can using the "Create a State of Focused Perception" practice. Then, focus your awareness on the heart center, at the center of your chest, and keep your focus there.

Begin to imagine what your heart looks like in your chest as it pumps blood. Continue to focus until you can see, sense, or feel your physical heart directly in front of you.

In your mind, move around to the back of your heart so that you can now see the back of your heart directly in front of you. Look for a fold or a crevice on your heart big enough for you to enter. Feel yourself moving closer to the place where you might enter. Now enter into the fold in whatever way is most comfortable.

Feel yourself falling until you suddenly stop so that you are standing up inside in a tiny, secret chamber inside your heart. See light if you want there to be light. Turn your attention to sensing what is going on around you, the motion and the sound.

Begin to recall feelings of love or gratitude, and express these feelings with your heart by picturing someone you love, such as your spouse, family member, or pet.

Think of something you would like to occur for your loved one, such as getting the job they want, recovering from illness, or finding a life partner.

Keep your focus on the heart center in your chest, looking down at the area with your eyes still closed. When you feel ready, open your eyes.

15

Death

Never Run Out of Time

Trained as an economist and psychotherapist, my scientifically-minded mother was generally less open to spiritual explanations than I am. A few years ago, as she became sick with cancer and close to death, we talked more about what death might be like. I told her I believed death would be like going out-of-body, where you become free of your body but you still know that you are you. I told her she may still be in the room after she died and might even be able to manipulate electricity—she could put on a show, if she wanted to. She didn't agree. I finally just told her, "If it's not true, don't worry about it. But if it might be, just think about it, okay?"

My mother died very early one morning in her own home, with my brother, who is a physician, his wife, my sister, and me present. After my brother announced she was gone, we stayed with her in her bedroom for a couple of hours. Later, we left the bedroom to return to the living room. Immediately upon leaving the bedroom, the radio next to her bed switched on at full volume. "I've been here for days," my brother said, "and that radio has not gone on once." His wife added, "The television just reset itself, like it was turning on." The next morning, my mother's medical alert pendant sent out an alarm to the central office as though someone was pressing on it. But it had remained by her bedside after her body had been taken away, in her locked home. I just laughed. My mother may have indeed given us a show.

Science hasn't definitively proven that whatever animates human brains continues after death, but according to studies, 4.2 percent of Americans have experienced a near-death experience, or NDE. This suggests that about fifteen million people may have experienced something akin to being conscious after a death incident.[1] This number is probably far higher because most people, myself included, do not immediately report these types of experiences and often wait years to reveal what they believe they experienced. Most of us have at least either heard stories of people who have felt the presence of others who have died or have ourselves sensed those presences.

While common wisdom suggests that extraordinary experiences like these are an aspect of mourning, there may be more to it. Death is generally defined as the irreversible cessation of vital body functions, including those carried out by the heart, respiratory system, and brain. But recently researchers called that definition into question by reanimating the brains of pigs after they had been dead for hours. Using a solution that mimicked blood flow, researchers pumped the brains full of oxygen and nutrients. They discovered that even though long dead and removed from the pigs' bodies, the brain cells resumed normal functioning, allowing neurons to carry electrical signals.[2]

Closely related to death experiences are out-of-body experiences, or OBEs. While researchers have historically avoided what might be considered fringe science, the phenomenon has recently gained serious attention. In fact, surveys report that about 10 percent of people, when asked, say they have had an experience of OBE at least once.

But to prove OBEs are real (i.e., able to be measured), someone would have to experience an OBE in a lab setting. That occurred recently when researchers at the University of Ottawa in Canada studied the brain of someone hooked up to brain imaging equipment while the person was having an "extra-corporeal experience."[3] The person having the OBE claimed to have had this ability since childhood. While the brain was being monitored during the OBE experience, researchers saw activity in an area suspected to be responsible for self-awareness. This part of the brain, called the temporoparietal junction, collects and processes information from someone's external senses as well as from within the body.

While the sensation of OBE is fairly well documented in people with brain anomalies, it hasn't been as well studied in healthy people. Research continues, with University College London researchers having also published a paper claiming the ability to induce an OBE in a lab setting.[4]

Regardless of how an OBE is triggered, the science explaining OBE mostly revolves around the idea that the brain is simply being tricked in a way that triggers its sense of self-awareness. This theory of OBE flies in the face of reports of people who are able to verify that they are still in the room after clinical death by recounting details they could not otherwise have known. Called "veridical perception," these types of reports remain controversial because data is sparse, incidents are difficult to replicate, and nothing can truly be proven beyond anecdotal observations. There is one famous verified case, however, which involved a brain-surgery patient named Pam Reynolds.[5] Reynolds, after an invasive brain operation to remove a tumor, was able to describe the procedure about which she could know nothing since she was clinically dead at the time and later revived. Just how Reynolds could have maintained self-awareness, normally associated with brain function, after she was clinically dead is still a mystery.

One explanation for Reynolds and the millions of people who report experiencing consciousness after death or OBE may be quantum entanglement and what is called "nonlocal consciousness." Nonlocal consciousness is the theory that human consciousness is not confined to specific, physical locations such as brains, bodies, and moments in time. Quantum entanglement, now proven to exist in biology, is being suggested as the mechanism behind nonlocal consciousness.[6] If consciousness is not a product of the physical brain and is instead due to some other phenomenon like quantum entanglement, then that may allow it to exist outside of or even after the death of the body.

If we were able to have an out-of-body experience at will, would we even want to? According to William Buhlman of the Monroe Institute, the benefits of out-of-body exploration extend far beyond the limits of our physical senses and our intellect. After an out-of-body experience, many people report an inner awakening of their spiritual identity and a transformation of their self-concept. They see themselves as more than matter—more aware and alive.[7] Other benefits of OBEs reported worldwide in the last many decades include greater awareness of reality, personal verification of one's immortality, accelerated personal development, decreased fear of death, increased psychic abilities, spontaneous healing, recognizing and experiencing past-life influences, increased intelligence, improved memory recall, and enhanced imagination.

Although many report lasting positive effects resulting from OBEs, those who experience them rarely talk about them. For example, here is Elena's account of what she believes was an out-of-body experience while driving on the Autobahn:

> I was eighteen years old, living in Germany, and I had received my driver's license. One evening, I decided to drive on the German Autobahn for only the third time. German Autobahns always have three lanes—slow on the right, medium in the middle, and fast on the left. Because I didn't feel very confident in my driving skills, I chose the slowest lane.
>
> Suddenly, I saw the car in front of me hit another car. I was shocked because I didn't think I could slow down in time to avoid crashing into it. I needed to change lanes. But as I looked to my left, I realized that another car was gaining on me in the middle lane. I couldn't turn out of my lane, and I couldn't stop in time. Either way, I thought, I was going to hit a car.
>
> A moment later, I felt this strange sensation come over me like I was hypnotized. It felt like my eyes were no longer open but closed shut, followed by a spinning inside my head. Then I sensed nothing, as though I were in no-man's-land and suspended in time. Another moment later, my eyes opened so that I could see again, and I was driving in the furthest left lane—two lanes away from where I had just been. There was no way I could have driven there myself because I would have hit that other car. I had no memory of crossing the middle lane to get there. I found myself thinking, *How is this possible? How did this just happen?*

It was like my car was airlifted and placed in the farthest left lane while I was still driving it.

During all of it, however, I wasn't afraid. Instead, I felt a sense of slowed-down time. In the split second while it was happening, I weighed in slow motion my two options of either crashing into the car in front of me or running into the car on the side of me. Then, when I couldn't see what was happening because I was in no-man's-land, that moment felt suspended in time. I felt like I had left my body and simply wasn't present for whatever happened. It wasn't until time resumed as normal that I felt the shock of being alive, unhurt, and driving with no car in front of me.

While there was no rational explanation for what happened, the fact that it did happen gave me a deep sense of joy and blissful relief. It was like a connection to a higher power. This feeling of being watched over and protected has never left me, even though to this day I can't explain it. One more thing: I didn't tell people right away because I didn't know what to say and because I was fairly young at the time. I thought people would either not believe me or ridicule me.

Elena was clearly experiencing a state of focused perception brought on by grave danger. Much like athletes in the state of flow and the common experience of time slowing down during life-threatening episodes, the brain may spontaneously generate multiple brainwave states like beta (alertness), alpha (mentally relaxed), theta (mindfulness), and gamma (peak focus) in order to cope with extraordinary circumstances. Out-of-body experiences are unique because they combine stretching and bending time, as Elena experienced, with a personal verification of one's immortality and decreased fear of death.

Below is a practice you can use to see whether you can travel outside your own body. If consciousness is not limited to the body but is somehow nonlocal and exists without it, then consciousness may continue after our body dies. Death may not be the end of life, and time may be even less limited than we thought.

PRACTICE:
NEVER RUN OUT OF TIME

To prepare yourself, plan to start at night. Successful out-of-body experiences are related to sleep cycles. With your body asleep and your mind still active, you are ripe for an out-of-body experience.

Prepare a place in your home beforehand that will be comfortable and safe to move to late at night to begin your OBE practice. Certain recorded music or guided visualizations can help greatly as you allow your body to fall asleep. Also, the use of the memory-enhancing supplement galantamine can help you lucidly dream and possibly trigger an out-of-body experience.[8] Of course, before taking this or any other supplement, seek your doctor's advice.

About three to three-and-a-half hours after you fall asleep, wake yourself up and move to the place you chose. A reclining lounge chair is ideal. Recline slightly in the chair or sofa but do not fully lie down.

Repeat the words "lose time" to yourself over and over in your mind's voice to focus your perception. Continue repeating the words until you lose conscious awareness.

If you have a vivid dream where it seems like you are somewhere else in the room, think of exiting out of the nearest door to get as far away from where you fell asleep as possible.

Note: It probably won't happen right away, and it will take practice, but an OBE is truly the gateway to effortlessly experience time as whatever you need it to be.

16

Immortality

Transcend Time

I n his book *Return to Life: Extraordinary Cases of Children Who Remember Past Lives*, Jim Tucker shares the story of Patrick, a five-year-old boy who was able to recall the life and experiences of his half-brother Kevin. Kevin, however, died twelve years before Patrick was born. Patrick is reported to remember swimming with his cousin, having surgery around the ear, and playing with his puppy, experiences Kevin had but Patrick had not. Remarkably, this connection seemed to extend to Patrick's physical body as well, with three birthmarks found almost precisely where tumors or scars had existed on Kevin's body during his lifetime.[1] Although Patrick's story is unusual because the life he remembers was so long ago, Tucker's book reports many other experiences of children who seem to remember events they should not be able to recall because they never experienced them.

These reports came after Tucker interviewed twenty-five hundred children, most of them under the age of six. A psychiatry professor at UVA Medical School, Tucker controversially concluded that the most scientific explanation for these children's experiences is that they are actually recalling their own past lives. Moreover, interesting trends emerged from the data collected from thousands of cases studied by Tucker. For example, about 70 percent of the children reported dying as a result of a violent or unnatural death, 90 percent of children reported being the same sex in their current life as they were in their previous life, and the interval between the death of the child and the birth into a new body averaged about sixteen months.

How could this happen? One speculative theory is that life may not be so much biological, but informational. Think of "information" as a fact about something's properties or existence. In physics, matter and energy are believed to be what makes up the universe. Recently, scientists in a field called quantum information processing are theorizing that the universe may instead be an immense *system* that processes information—a computer—that gives rise to matter and energy, and not the other way around.[2] Their argument is as follows: because (1) the universe is made up of atoms as well as other elementary particles; (2) the subatomic particles that make up atoms interact with one another according to the laws of quantum mechanics; and (3) when they interact information is generated; therefore, (4) what makes up the universe is information. Think of when an ocean wave comes ashore. Every water molecule brings information to the wave, such as its position relative to other molecules. When two water molecules interact, they change position or move around as a result of "processing" that information. With countless numbers of water molecules interacting with one another, the result is the wave. If this kind of scenario were taking place in the human brain, the result could be a thought, suggesting consciousness.

Another theory that applies principles of quantum computing to how thoughts are formed by the brain as consciousness comes from a giant in the field of physics, physicist Roger Penrose.[3] The theory suggests that the brain may house quantum states in the form of neural activity that exist in multiple states at once—either "on" or "off"—because of quantum superposition. As such, they are like the bits of information in a quantum computer that are themselves either "on" or "off." Then, in an instant, the neural activity comes together in a single, quantum event we experience as a conscious thought. Most mainstream scientists, however, do not see how this could be a possible explanation. The "quantum coherence" Penrose is suggesting is typically extremely environmentally and temperature sensitive, and doesn't happen outside of highly-protected circumstances. Scientists argue that the brain is too wet and warm for quantum processes to play any role there.

Still, Penrose remains convinced that in order to explain the brain and consciousness, we are going to have to throw out our notion that neuroscience, biology, or even physics can explain what is going on.

Whether our brains and consciousness are the result of quantum computers that generate information, or of quantum fields where large number of particles interact in ways quantum theory allows, conservation of energy is real—meaning nothing is ever created or destroyed, just changed from one form to another. That same principle of nothing being created or destroyed could explain the seeming immortality of Tucker's past-life children. In the world of classical physics, information can be deleted at will. But in the quantum world, the theory of conservation of quantum information means that information can neither be created nor destroyed.[4] If true, then the quantum information about the deceased children's lives could live on in other children.

The practical implications are mind-boggling. As just one example, the secret to immortality would not necessarily be to make the physical body live forever. The secret of immortality would be that everyone and everything are *already* immortal, as a result of quantum information that may never die out. So often we feel like we don't have enough time to do what we need to do, believing that time is our enemy. The reality may be quite different: time is less limited than we think. If we can sense that our immortal nature extends beyond time, we can instead feel as though we have all the time in the world.

Still, questions about what life is and how something that is "alive" differs from inanimate matter, or something that is not "alive," remain. Centuries ago, philosophers and scientists theorized that living organisms were somehow made alive by spirit, or a "spark" of life that is missing from inanimate matter. By the nineteenth century, advances in science resulted in a significant shift away from that previously held view: organisms are made up of molecules, which are made up of atoms, which are subject to chemistry, physics, and the laws of thermodynamics, which bring it to life. As such, living organisms at the molecular level may be no different from, for example, steam engines that work as a result of the thermodynamic reactions. Living organisms are just extraordinarily more complex.

In the twentieth century, however, something remarkable happened. The mysterious, fantastic world of quantum mechanics was discovered, which had its own set of laws: quantum particles are collapsed from wave functions as a result of observation, can exist in multiple states at once, and exhibit spooky connections to one another even across huge distances. With the old ways of thinking about physics increasingly eclipsed by the new scientific frontier ahead, one of the giants of quantum mechanics, Erwin Schrödinger (Remember Schrödinger's cat?), attempted to answer the question *What is life?* for himself. In his 1944 book by that name, Schrödinger suggested that how cells behave and nervous systems work can be explained by already-discovered and yet-to-be discovered laws of physics: cells are part of statistical systems, the mutations of cells are like quantum leaps, and entropy affects the way things decay and fall apart.[5] Nearly a century later, advances in science have provided quantum-based explanations for such fundamental biological processes as photosynthesis, enzymatic chemical reactions, and migratory bird navigation. Maybe Schrödinger and the many other scientists continuing to explore questions that are not yet answered will one day answer the question completely.

In the meantime, I use the next practice to get in touch with my immortal nature. Whenever I feel paralyzed by a thought or feeling that is keeping me from being completely present or taking action, I use this practice to trigger a transcendent, self-surpassing experience of singularity, or unity consciousness, typically associated with gamma brainwaves, believed to indicate the highest state of consciousness. By intentionally triggering this state, I am virtually guaranteed to be liberated from whatever thought or feeling that was paralyzing me so I can once again feel timeless.

Using this practice, you may for a moment experience that everything you think of as separate from you is instead indistinguishable from you. After all, everything that makes up the universe, including matter, is simply quantum particles interacting with one another and generating information according to a theory of everything, where reality may be one part physical and one part perception. In this state, all feelings of worry and fear can vanish and become replaced with feelings of timelessness.

PRACTICE:
TRANSCEND TIME

Relax as deeply as you can using the "Create a State of Focused Perception" practice. Now, abruptly open your eyes. Look around you. Think this thought: *Everything is me.*

Hold this thought for as long as you can, even as your logical mind starts chattering. When your thoughts drift, once again think this thought: *Everything is me.* Include everything around you in your thought: the chair, the computer, the desk, the book—everything.

See how long you can focus your mind before your brain begins to bombard you with thoughts that interrupt your focus. Use your will to reintroduce the idea that *everything around you is you.*

Advanced Technique:
Enhancing the Experience

Look around you and imagine that everywhere you look you see yourself. There is no separation. Then imagine that you are seeing yourself in all that is around you and you are the creator of it. There may be boundaries you sense between you and, for instance, the table, but in some sense they are artificial. The atoms and subatomic particles that make up your body and the table are no different. Look deeper at your hand and at the table and imagine those boundaries do not exist.

17

A Suggested
Daily Practice for
Transcending Time

Now that you have updated your construct of time and know some ways to practically apply it, what's next? How can you put everything together into something you can do daily to change your experience of time? Here is one suggestion for combining the science of time with your own personal transformation work as a daily practice.

1. Morning Practice

Each morning, begin your day with the practice of focused perception (chapter 6). Then ask yourself, *What is mine to do today?*

Based on what you learn by asking yourself this question, write down the day's top priorities. Make the choice to prioritize these things above all else as you go about your day, trusting that whatever comes up will advance these priorities. Then, remind yourself of this: *Time is one part physical and one part perception. I can change my perception of any event at any moment by focusing on it.*

2. Throughout the Day

The second key to transcending time is remaining in the present moment. During the day, if you feel overwhelmed, panicked, or pressed for time, stop what you are doing, find a quiet place, and use the practice of focused perception (chapter 6) to return to the present moment.

If you still have trouble staying in the present moment, regrets from the past may be getting in the way. Use the "Reverse the Past" practice (chapter 8) to free yourself from these paralyzing thoughts.

Similarly, if worry, anxiety, or fear of the future is keeping you from remaining in the present moment, use the practice of "Don't Let the Future Slow You Down" and the "What's True?" advanced technique (chapter 9) to be free from those thoughts.

3. In Case of Emergency

- When you're running late for an important meeting: "Stretch Time" (chapter 10)

- When you need to complete an urgent task: "Receive Insight When You Need It" (chapter 11)

- When you need someone to contact you or you don't have time to contact them directly: "Reach Others Fast" (chapter 12)

- When you need to know someone or something is safe and you don't have time to travel there in person: "Instantly Verify What Matters Most" to your current situation (chapter 13)

- When someone you care about needs something: "Harness Metaphysical Gravity" (chapter 14)

- When you feel overwhelmed by your current circumstances and need a quick reminder that time is not your enemy: "Transcend Time" (chapter 16)

4. Evening Practice

Before going to sleep each night, "Reverse the Past" (chapter 8) to free yourself from the past. Also, if you feel gripped by a sense of worry or fear, use the "Don't Let the Future Slow You Down" practice with the "What's True?" technique (chapter 9).

For more resources and support for developing your own ongoing practice of transcending time and doing what is yours to do, see allthetimebook.com.

Conclusion

On June 30, 2016, while living in Florida, I was walking on a local beach as I often did on summer afternoons. As I began to leave, a police vehicle entered the beach from the street, which was a little unusual because there seemed to be no reason to do so. As I watched the vehicle navigate the uneven sand, something else caught my eye. In what I can only describe as a momentary vision, I "saw" the word "police" on the side of the vehicle somehow transform into the words "peace officer."

Later at home, I thought about what I had seen. Maybe something as simple as changing the words people see on police vehicles to "peace officer" was more powerful than it seemed at first glance. After all, "peace officer" is how local laws usually refer to police of all kinds around the country. It was the one fundamental term that united police officers everywhere.

That was exactly four years before June 2020, when a series of national events shone a light on the issue of how the police view their role in communities versus how citizens wanted to be policed. With that said, any one of us could have taken notice even four years ago if we'd really thought about the trend of growing conflict between the police and communities.

It occurred to me that the disconnect both for police and community members was the perceived role of the police. Maybe if we could just change the way police saw themselves and the way the citizens saw them, we could change the dynamic of what was going on around the country. As a result of my background in economics, where I was taught to test theories in real-world situations, I decided to do just that. Guess what? It turned out to be true. Something as simple as changing the way police and citizens think of themselves does change the dynamic; it reimagines the conversation.

I eventually formed the national nonprofit Police2Peace, which today unites police departments and communities around the country in ways that uplift and heal them, including introducing the words "peace offi-cer" into the conversation. The formation of Police2Peace has been called "ridiculously timely."

I have no police officers in my family and no history of law enforce-ment training or advocacy. Instead, the vision for Police2Peace came to me in an instant when I "saw" the words appear in front of my eyes. After that, my life was forever transformed. I became committed to the cause of criminal justice reform and continue to advocate for change on a national level. The question I am asked most often about this experience is, *How did you know what to do next?* My answer to that is contained in these pages. Because of the practices I've included in this book, I've been able to more easily recognize what is mine to do and to do it.

With our daily lives inextricably interwoven with and dependent upon time, we believe that without the passage of time, virtually noth-ing of our lives would exist. Time defines our experience of physical reality. However, we have now learned that time is not just physical, but also based in our perceptions. When we focus our perception, we change our experience of time. When we change our experience of time, we transcend time, and therefore master it. When we master time, we master ourselves.

My question for you is, *What is yours to do?*

Acknowledgments

For all my partners in time who made this body of work possible, especially Don, Amanda, Steve, Jan, Diana, and the Sounds True team: thank you for your inspiration, expertise, and artistry. For my dedicated contributors and readers, especially Marcia, Lore, Devon, Anitra, Charlie, Elena, Anthony, Jules, Terry, Ben, Bill, Rich, Martha, Lana, Hunter, Stephen, Gordon, Lori, Lidia, Barbara, Pete, Meryl, Claudette, Dru, Evangeline, Patty, Mike, Patrick, Veronica, Philsha, Ross, Leslie, Joanie, Debra, Marci, Jack, don Miguel, Bruce, Dean, Roger, Ori, Henry, George, David, Constance, Charlotte, Chris, Nick, Katy, Amy, Anne, Peter, and Laura: thank you for your honesty, thoughtfulness, and countless hours spent. For Donald Carlin, PhD, educated at MIT and Yale in physics: thank you for keeping me on the straight and narrow. For Arthur, Jim, and Scott, for believing anything is possible. For Tony, who has always supported me. And for Jerry, I'm sure you're here somewhere.

Appendix A
Additional Science

Throughout this book, claims—that might be regarded by some as extraordinary—have been made to support certain arguments and theories. Here you will find additional science in support of those claims.

Wave-Particle Duality

We know that quantum physicists study particles even smaller than atoms and that they don't seem to behave in the same way as the large things we can see, feel, and hold—but do you know how they discovered these mysterious particles and the laws that govern their behavior?

Before quantum science was even an idea, Thomas Young announced in 1803 that light had properties that could only be explained if it had the properties of a wave. Over a hundred years later, Albert Einstein proved that certain frequencies of light also existed as "discrete packets of energy," like particles of light called "photons." He won the 1921 Nobel Prize for his theory. These two theories were thought to apply only to light until Louis de Broglie's 1924 doctoral thesis theorized that electrons, as well as everything else—matter, electrons, and atoms—could have the properties of both waves and particles. De Broglie won the 1929 Nobel Prize for this idea. That opened the door to the first theory of quantum physics commonly called *wave-particle duality*, one of the most famous concepts in quantum theory.

Wave-particle duality refers to the idea that light, and matter in general, can behave as both a wave and a particle. Thomas Young, Albert Einstein, and many others after them used the same type of experiment to demonstrate the wave and particle properties of photons, commonly called the double-slit experiment.

Here's how it worked. First, a screen with a single slit cut through it was placed between the light (photon) source and a plate meant to record where the photons landed. Light was emitted from the source, like tiny photon bullets being shot out of a gun. As a result of all those bullet-like photons piling up, a fuzzy image was created by the photons that went through the slit in the screen and hit the plate behind it. The fact that they piled up on the plate at the other end indicated that the photons were behaving like particles. (See the image in chapter 8.)

Not satisfied with that result, these early physics pioneers experimented with what might happen if they cut two slits in the screen.[1] Remember, they were trying to shoot just one photon, which they assumed to be a solid single particle, so you might think that the single photon would go through just one slit. Or you might think that they would get two images of piled-up photons, matching the two slits. They didn't get either of those. Instead, the light appeared to pass through *both* slits at the same time. And rather than behaving like a photon particle, the images on the other side of the slits looked like waves. Specifically, they ended up looking like the two separate sets of intersecting waves that had interfered with one another, like two bullets shot into a pond, where the ripples from each impact extend out and interfere with each other.

The Observer Effect

So, why were these photons behaving like particles in the single-slit experiments and like waves in the double-slit experiments? To learn more, scientists set up sensors to observe the photons as they traveled through the two slits to hit the plate behind the screen. Here's what happened: When observed by a sensor, each photon behaved as though it had gone through just *one* of the slits. In other words, the wave pattern on the photographic plate disappeared, and they got what they originally expected: photons that looked like particles instead of waves on the other side of the slit. As strange as it seemed, only when the photon was observed by the sensor as going through one slit or the other did its behavior change from that of a wave to that of a particle. Also, the photons either behaved like a particle *or* a wave; scientists were not able to observe them behaving like particles and waves at the same time. And although this debate started with a photon, remember that wave-particle duality is not limited to just photons. Similar experiments have been done with everything from neutrons to atoms to even larger molecules.[2]

Scientists have performed the photon experiment numerous times since then, but also with a twist. In what became known as the "quantum eraser" experiment, they devised ways to intentionally not observe the photon. In each case, they found that observing the absence of a photon had the same effect as observing the presence of it.[3] Since nothing was actually observed and only the absence of observation occurred, this suggested that the observation itself was the critical process in wave function collapse. As Professor Richard Conn Henry wrote in the journal *Nature*, "The wave function is collapsed simply by your human mind seeing nothing." This led him to conclude, "The universe is entirely mental."[4]

Quantum Entanglement in the Physical World

As mentioned in chapter 3, researchers are actively working to demonstrate that the quantum principles governing the microscopic world may also apply to the macroscopic world to result in a theory of everything. One way scientists are attempting to merge general relativity with quantum mechanics is using the concept of entanglement.

Recall that when particles are entangled with one another, they behave as though they are connected, even if they are separated by great distances like the entire universe. Recently, this was successfully demonstrated by researchers from Brookhaven National Laboratory, Stony Brook University, and DOE's Energy Sciences Network (ESnet) with entangled photons separated by eleven miles. This is believed to be one of the longest-distance entanglement experiments in the United States.[5] On an even larger scale, researchers now suggest that quantum entanglement and space-bound wormholes are the same phenomena.[6] Ordinarily, physicists describe quantum entanglement as existing only between two particles. But in a recent paper, researchers suggest that the explanation for the behavior of entangled subatomic particles is that they may be connected by a kind of quantum wormhole. In fact, spacetime itself might come from quantum entanglement. Since wormholes are distortions of space described by Einstein's gravitation, researchers now understand that many particles, governed by quantum mechanics, can be entangled. Moreover, identifying wormholes that normally only exist in astrophysics with quantum entanglement would be a solid link between general relativity and quantum mechanics.

Quantum Superposition in the Physical World

In their pursuit of a theory of everything, some researchers have also been focusing on the concept of superposition. Just recently an international team of scientists studying time suggested that time can flow in a way that is genuinely quantum.[7] We already know from physical laws that the presence of massive objects slows down time due to gravity. This means that a clock placed close to a massive object will run slower compared to an identical clock that is farther away. So why can't this same effect exist in the microscopic quantum world? For example, how would a clock keep time if it were affected by an immense object in the quantum world?

Although the vast majority of physicists hope otherwise, the traditional scientific answer is that the scenario is not conceivable. This is because, in the macroscopic world governed by general relativity, events are continuous and subject to cause and effect, meaning every cause matches up to an effect. In the microscopic world of quantum mechanics, however, things happen as a result of probabilities rather than cause and effect. Remember wave-particle duality, and the possibility of Schrödinger's cat existing in two different states, called the superposition state.

What might happen if an object so immense that its gravity can warp time were put in a quantum superposition scenario—therefore combining quantum principles and physical laws in a single scenario? Researchers asking the question came up with this thought experiment. Think of two starships on a mission in space: ship 1 and ship 2. They have been instructed to shoot weapons at one another at exactly the same moment and afterward fly away to avert the other's weapon fire. At this moment, they are considered to be in superposition to one another, meaning they exist as possibly being both shot and not shot at the same time.

Now let's introduce gravity into the experiment. Imagine that an immense object, like a planet, was nearer to ship 1 than ship 2. From the vantage point of ship 1, time would appear to speed up for ship 2 to the point that its time would appear to be passing more quickly. Remember our black hole example from prior chapters. As a result, ship 2, the ship more distant from the planet, will always get to the moment it is instructed to shoot its weapons faster than ship 1. And ship 1 will never have the opportunity to fire quickly enough to hit ship 2, which sets up an indisputable order of events in time. The superposition of the ships, a uniquely quantum phenomenon, when combined with the effect of gravity on the ships, a uniquely physical phenomenon, means that two "worlds" can coexist, at least in theory, in the real world.[8] So although this is a thought experiment and not an actual battle in space, it's not science fiction.

Consciousness Causes Collapse in the Physical World

Other groundbreaking research has tried to show the effect of our intentions in our everyday world to suggest that consciousness causes collapse for physical things we can sense. For decades, the output of quantum-based random number generators has been used to determine whether nonrandom results as a result of human intention could be proven. Subjects of these types of experiments are told to cause, for example, one light on a panel to illuminate more than another using their thoughts. The lights, or whatever signal is being used, would otherwise be generated randomly by the quantum random number generator. If the subjects' thoughts had no effect on the random number generator, 50 percent of the lights would always be one color and 50 percent would always be the other color. In a recent meta-analysis, however, a small but uniform deviation from chance was shown to exist across all the studies, suggesting a role of intentional human observation might exist for physical matter.[9]

This body of research is called *micro-psychokinesis*. It attempts to measure, using the physics of the macroscopic world, a phenomenon that is believed to only occur in the microscopic quantum world: consciousness causes collapse of the wave function. While research like this continues to be published,[10] the scientific community in general remains unconvinced, even with large amounts of supporting data being aggregated across numerous studies. This skepticism illustrates another of the biggest problems in physics today: the apparent difference between how large, macroscopic objects behave and how tiny, microscopic particles behave.

But what if the concept of consciousness causes collapse is simply another way of describing the psychokinetic manipulation of matter that physicists have not fully accounted for? After all, this idea is not new. Human beings have been fascinated by the possibility of a mind-body connection manifesting in physical reality for millennia. Ancient spiritual traditions, as well as most world religions, mythologies, and philosophies, all incorporate aspects of this belief. For example, Eastern spiritual traditions going back thousands of years, such as in China and India, have traditionally believed that the mind plays an essential role in healing the body. These cultures and many others, such as Mesopotamia, Egypt, Greece, Rome, and Judaism, also believed that the human mind was able to create or change aspects of physical reality.

These beliefs continued for centuries until the Renaissance of the fourteenth and fifteenth centuries. At that time, primarily Western philosophers began debating about whether the mind and mental phenomena were physical or nonphysical in nature. In the seventeenth century, one of the most famous of these philosophers, René Descartes, first identified the mind with consciousness and the brain with the body, effectively "splitting" the mind away from brain, which was considered to be the physical source of intelligence. Now referred to as the Cartesian mind-body split, this suggestion that human beings are dual in nature—one part mind and one part body—persists as the dominant belief in Western culture to this day. Nevertheless, in his own musings, Descartes wrote about how gambling outcomes could be influenced by the mood of the gambler.[11] Three hundred years later, more scientific investigation into the connection between mind and matter used dice tosses.[12] Since then, large numbers of studies have been performed to consider the possibility of mentally-induced changes to inanimate objects performed by humans, such as throwing dice, throwing coins—and random number generators.

Paralleling these real-world experiences and experiments are more recent, theoretical experiments indicating that the quantum process of consciousness causes collapse may be another way of describing the psychokinetic manipulation of matter. In one study, the observer effect is described as quantum entanglement between the intentional observer and what is being observed.[13] In another study by physicist Roger Penrose, the "observation" is a transfer of unconscious knowledge of something in the quantum world into a conscious experience of its precise existence.[14] Penrose supposes that consciousness isn't computational—meaning it isn't able to be reduced to a machine. Moreover, it's beyond what even neuroscience or biology can explain. Using the theory of quantum computing, however, Penrose theorizes that momentary thoughts come together in what is known as *quantum coherence*, where they suddenly act together in one quantum state, resulting in consciousness. These moments of consciousness are made possible by special wiring in the brain, which is believed to store and process both information and memory.

As this evidence of consciousness causes collapse accumulates, one can't help but ask the question: At what point can we say physics is proving the existence of consciousness itself?

Given the relentless focus of science on proving a theory of everything and the progress made so far, experiments on increasingly large things where quantum theories hold up, and a theoretically viable theory of everything, seem inevitable.

Appendix B

A Compilation of Practices

Create a State of Focused Perception[1]

1. Practice this one in darkness, whether it's by closing your eyes, turning off the lights, or wearing an eye mask.

2. Sit comfortably on the floor with your legs folded in front of you (commonly called the lotus position) and rest your hands on your lap with your palms up. If this posture is uncomfortable, sit on a small pillow with your legs folded in front of you, or sit against a wall with your legs stretched out in front of you.

3. Notice your mind working: Is it reflecting on something that happened in the past? Is it planning for something to happen in the future? Is it noticing something around you?

4. Simply allow the thoughts to occur as they come to you.

5. Turn your focus to your breath. Begin to inhale through your nose and exhale through your mouth, with your exhaled breath twice as long as your inhaled breath. Imagine your exhalation as smoke or mist leaving your mouth.

6. With your next exhale, see the numeral 3 appear before your closed eyes.

7. With your next exhale, see the numeral 3 change to the numeral 2.

8. With your next exhale, see the numeral 2 change to the numeral 1.

9. With your next exhale, see the numeral 1 change to the numeral 0.

10. Remain in this state of quiet, focused perception for as long as you want.

11. When you feel ready, slowly open your eyes, or continue with another practice.

Advanced Technique: Puppies and Kittens

1. When any conscious thought comes to mind, focus on the thought.

2. Turn it into something you love, like a puppy or a kitten.

3. Intentionally take that puppy or kitten and put them "outside." This will have the effect of removing them from your awareness.

4. If they return, just put them outside again, until they no longer return.

Advanced Technique: What Is Mine to Do Today?

1. When in this state of focused perception, instead of opening your eyes right away, you can ask yourself a question you'd like to know the answer to, such as, *What is mine to do today?*

2. When you have received the clarity or sense of completion you need, slowly open your eyes.

Experience Your Life in Advance

1. Relax as deeply as you can, using the "Create a State of Focused Perception" practice.

2. Think of something you would really like to create for yourself. I recommend choosing something that benefits everyone involved and doesn't harm or detract from anyone or anything.

3. Imagine that what you want to create has already occurred in every sense: visually, experientially, and emotionally. Put out of your mind any explanation for how it has happened; simply accept that it is done and complete.

4. Immerse yourself deeply in the sensations of what has been created as well as the feeling of relief or satisfaction that it is already accomplished. If you're having trouble feeling what you want is already created,

imagine you are diving into the feeling like a giant lake. See yourself bathing in it, so the sensations permeate every cell of your body.

5. When you are ready, slowly open your eyes.

Advanced Technique: Dream Your Life Three Years in Advance

1. Relax as deeply as you can using the "Create a State of Focused Perception" practice.

2. Imagine seeing yourself from afar, seated exactly as you are right now. Now, imagine a bubble surrounds you and lifts you up from wherever you are seated so that you are now seeing your home, office building, or other current location below you.

3. Imagine the bubble beginning to move to your right as you see the Earth move by below you. Continue to imagine the bubble moving until you sense you have moved three years into the future. See the bubble stop and lower you back down to Earth. Notice your surroundings. Where are you? What are you doing? Who are you with? Do not feel you must create what you are experiencing; simply notice it. By imagining yourself three years in the future, you can get a sense of what you want to create for yourself and your life.

4. Once you have made note of your life three years in advance, imagine the bubble again surrounding you and lifting you up. See the Earth move underneath you as you imagine the bubble now moving to your left. When you sense you are two years in advance—meaning you have gone back in time one year from where you just were—imagine the bubble putting you down. You are in your life as you imagine it two years from now. What do you see?

5. See the bubble surround you again and lift you up. See the Earth move underneath you as you imagine the bubble again moving to your left, this time traveling to the time one year in the future. Imagine the bubble lowering you down to Earth once more. What do you see now?

6. And finally, travel back to the present time so that you're sitting exactly where you are right now. Write down what you saw, including any insights about the path it may take to get there.

Reverse the Past[2]

1. Relax as deeply as you can, using the "Create a State of Focused Perception" practice.

2. When you see the numeral 0 appear before your closed eyes, shift your focus to an experience in your life you want to change and rid yourself of. It could be a minor experience or something significant. If you sense there's a deeper trauma behind a minor event but aren't sure what it is, start with the minor event.

3. Begin to relive the sensations of where you were and who you were with. Bring up any emotions related to the experience, like anger, fear, resentment, frustration, sadness, or anxiety.

4. Welcome the negative emotions. Hold the experience and the emotions in your mind as though all of them were happening again to you right now, in the moment.

5. Now, reverse whatever you felt was negative about the experience so that instead it is fully resolved.

6. Allow all issues and questions surrounding the experience to dissolve from your thoughts.

7. Breathe a sigh of relief and feel fully empowered by the sense that the issue is resolved.

8. When you are ready, slowly open your eyes.

Advanced Technique:
Reverse an Experience in Real Time

If you'd like to dissolve the negative effects of something you've just experienced, simply find a quiet place to sit and reverse it in real time.

Advanced Technique:
Reverse Your Day

1. As you lie in bed just before you fall asleep, think of the moment you first opened your eyes that morning.

2. Go through your day in your mind, changing each experience into the best possible version of what could have happened for you.

3. Continue to do that for all experiences you remember from your day until you have completely relived your day and you see yourself in your bed, ready to fall asleep.

Advanced Technique:
Reverse a Dream

If you wake up disturbed from a bad dream, follow the steps in the practice above, and instead of vividly reliving a past event, vividly relive your dream. When you get to the disturbing part, say to yourself, *That's not what happened*, and instead reverse the negative part so the best possible outcome happens instead.

Advanced Technique:
Reverse Past Trauma

1. If you are experiencing persistent negative emotions related to a particular scenario and you aren't sure why, *and* you are ready and willing to work on the deeper cause of your negative emotions, you can begin with the "Receive Insight When You Need It" practice (see page 147).

2. When you have a sense of what the source of your negative emotions might be, reverse it using the "Reverse the Past" practice.

3. When you get to the part where you see your situation resolved, imagine that your wisest, kindest adult self is now present with you in the event.

4. What was most needed in this moment to resolve or heal all these negative emotions? See your adult self providing it for you.

5. Feel all the positive emotions that occur now that the event is fully resolved in the best possible way.

6. Complete the remainder of the "Reverse the Past" practice as written above.

Don't Let the Future Slow You Down

1. Relax as deeply as you can using the "Create a State of Focused Perception" practice.

2. When you see the numeral 0 appear in front of your closed eyes, shift your focus to the fearful or worrisome thought that you want to neutralize and rid yourself of.

3. Begin to fully experience the emotion of fear by imagining in detail the unpleasant circumstances that would result in you or others being harmed. If you're experiencing a minor worry, intensify the worrisome thought to the extreme experience of all the unpleasant things that could happen.

4. Intensify the emotion of fear until you feel the sensations in your body. Hold the experience and the emotions in your mind as though all of them were happening to you right now, in the moment.

5. Now stop, and instead become aware that the experience never happened. Right now, in the moment, you are fine, there is no unpleasantness, you are completely safe.

6. Say to yourself, *Oh, that's not what happened at all*, or *It didn't happen that way*. Allow all thoughts and sensations you imagined might happen to dissolve from your mind. You don't know how or why, but just dive into the feeling of relief that the unpleasantness never happened in the way you imagined. Your mind may object, so just set that objection aside. If an objection comes up again, that's okay. Just continue to set those thoughts aside.

7. Feel fully free from the unpleasantness, which could include a sense of safety or a positive outcome. See yourself breathing a sigh of relief that the unpleasantness never happened.

8. When you are ready, slowly open your eyes.

Advanced Technique: What's True?[3]

1. To neutralize persistent recurring fears, use this practice with a partner.

2. Begin with the "Create a State of Focused Perception" practice.

3. Open your eyes and write down the bare facts of the situation, and at least two different interpretations of those facts.

4. If you were worried about losing your job, for example, have your partner begin by asking you, "So, you think you're going to lose your job. What's true?"

5. Respond with what's true by reading the two different interpretations.

6. Then your partner asks you again, "What's true?"

7. You again respond with two different interpretations of the facts.

8. Continue this back and forth until you begin to see the way your brain may have been distorting the facts of the situation to result in unpleasant interpretations of what might happen.

9. Eventually, you will uncover what is really true, which is likely to be not as unpleasant as you feared.

Stretch Time

1. Sit comfortably in front of a clock with a second hand and take note of the second hand's position.

2. Intermittently shift your eyes away from the clock as far to the left or right as you are able.

3. Repeatedly shift your eyes straight back to fixate directly on the clockface.

4. Begin to relive a vivid memory that is long and involved, like playing a wonderful movie back in your mind.

5. Focus on the clock, the second hand will appear not to have moved. In some cases, it moves backward.

Advanced Technique:
Be on Time (When Not Driving)

1. Gaze softly at the clock as a disinterested person would. Notice the monotonous rhythm of its movement or of the numbers changing.

2. Use your intention to shift your eyes straight back to fixate directly on the clockface.

3. Repeatedly shift your eyes away from the clock to the road or wherever else you are and then back on the clockface.

4. Begin to imagine a vivid scene of arriving at your destination on time, like playing a movie of it in your head.

5. Continue playing this movie of arriving on time for as long as you are traveling to your destination, intermittently shifting your eyes away from the clock to the road or your surroundings.

Advanced Technique:
Be on Time (When Driving)

1. Think about the positive benefits to you or others if you arrive on time.

2. Feel your positive desire to be on time in order to benefit all parties involved.

3. Then, let the desire go.

4. Create a movie in your mind of arriving to your destination on time, seeing all the positive outcomes of doing so.

5. Remind yourself that you have all the time in the world to get to where you need to go.

6. Imagine time stretching and shifting around you to make room for however long your journey needs to take.

7. Continue to replay that movie of arriving on time in your mind until you reach your destination.

Receive Insight When You Need It[4]

1. Sit comfortably where you can be undisturbed and under no time pressure. It's best if you're alone, although you don't need to be. It's also best if your eyes are closed and even better if you're in darkness. None of this is necessary; it simply optimizes your brain for receptivity.

2. Bring yourself into a meditative state using the "Create a State of Focused Perception" practice.

3. Ask yourself this question: *What do I myself know about this?* Insert the subject you want to know about at the end of the question, such as, *What do I myself know about this pain in my lower back?*

4. Sit quietly for as long as you want. Don't worry about not immediately getting an answer, although you will always get an answer of some kind that pops into your head.

5. When a thought, idea, image, or answer comes to you, remember what it is, such as, *I had an accident when I was ten years old.*

6. Repeat the question, this time inserting the answer into the end of the same question: *What do I myself know about this accident I had when I was ten years old?*

7. Wait for the new thought or answer, and again insert that thought or answer at the end of the same question.

8. Repeat this sequence of questions and answers until you feel you have more information than you did when you started.

Reach Others Fast

1. Begin by quieting yourself with the "Create a State of Focused Perception" practice.

2. Bring to mind a vivid scene of what you want to experience as a result of sending your message, such as answering your phone and it's the person you've been trying to reach, or looking at your email inbox and the email you've been waiting for is there unopened.

3. Visualize the person you want to receive your message. If you are far away from the receiver, it might be helpful to look at a picture of them before you begin visualizing them.

4. Call to mind the feelings you experience when you interact with the person face-to-face.

5. Feel these emotions as if the person were actually in your presence. Focus on these feelings, and believe that you are creating a connection with the other person.

6. Focus on a single image or word you want to hear or read.

7. Visualize it with as much detail as possible, and focus your mind solely on it. Concentrate on what it looks like, what it's like to touch it, and/or how it makes you feel.

8. After forming a clear mental image, transmit your message to the person by imagining the words or object traveling from your mind into the receiver's.

9. Visualize yourself face-to-face with the receiver, and say to them, "Cat," or whatever thought you're transmitting.

10. In your mind's eye, see the look of realization on their face as they understand what you're telling them.

11. Now become aware that what you want to happen has already occurred, completely, in every possible way.

12. Feel the sense of relief that there is nothing more to do. What you wanted to have done is already fully done. Let that sensation wash over your body, like diving into a giant lake, deeper and deeper.

13. When finished, abruptly stop and open your eyes.

Instantly Verify What Matters Most

1. In preparation for this practice, ask an assistant or friend to choose five to seven pictures to cut out from a magazine or download from the internet. These need to be pictures of real-world places that are iconic and known to you, like the Eiffel Tower, the Grand Canyon, or a big city. These will be your "targets." Ask them to place the pictures facedown in a stack in a sealed box or envelope.

2. When you're ready to begin, have blank paper and a pen or pencil next to you to write down your impressions.

3. Relax your body as deeply as you can using the "Create a State of Focused Perception" practice.

4. Begin to imagine how it would feel to be someplace else in your home or environment, such as being outside if you are indoors or in the bedroom if you are in your living room. The more relaxed you are, the more intently you will be able to focus on the feeling of being in another place.

5. Now imagine you are inside the box or envelope of pictures, looking down at the stack.

6. Turn over the first picture with your mind. Take in just basic impressions of what you are seeing. Try to notice what you feel is the most imposing image in the target: Is it natural or constructed? Is it on land or in the water? Write down the first thing you see.

7. Draw a sketch of the target. Really take the time to observe the colors and shapes of what you see.

8. Now imagine you are floating over the target several feet above it. Note on your paper your impressions about the target from above.

9. Write a brief summary of everything you saw. Include any information that comes to you in as much detail as possible while not judging anything. Be sure to include sensory information, like a smell, colors, a taste, the temperature, or blurry shapes and patterns. Note if you feel an emotional reaction to the target.

10. Remove the first photo from the stack and compare it to your impressions.

11. When ready, repeat these steps for each picture in the stack.

Harness Metaphysical Gravity[5]

1. Relax as deeply as you can using the "Create a State of Focused Perception" practice.

2. Focus your awareness in the heart center, at the center of your chest, and keep your focus there.

3. Begin to imagine what your heart looks like in your chest as it pumps blood. Continue to focus until you can see, sense, or feel your physical heart directly in front of you.

4. In your mind, move around to the back of your heart so that you can now see the back of your heart directly in front of you.

5. Look for a fold or a crevice on your heart big enough for you to enter.

6. Feel yourself moving closer to the place where you might enter.

7. Enter into the fold in whatever way is most comfortable.

8. Feel yourself falling until you suddenly stop so that you are standing up inside in a tiny, secret chamber inside your heart. See light if you want there to be light.

9. Turn your attention to sensing what is going on around you, the motion and the sound.

10. Begin to recall feelings of love or gratitude.

11. Express these feelings with your heart by picturing someone you love, such as your spouse, family member, or pet.

12. Think of something you would like to occur for your loved one, such as getting the job they want, recovering from illness, or finding a life partner.

13. Keep your focus on the heart center in your chest, looking down at the area with your eyes still closed.

14. When you feel ready, open your eyes.

Never Run Out of Time

1. Plan to start your OBE practice at night. Prepare a place in your home beforehand that will be comfortable and safe to move to late at night.

2. About three to three-and-a-half hours after you fall asleep, wake yourself up and move to the place you chose. A reclining lounge chair is ideal.

3. Recline slightly in the chair or sofa but do not fully lie down.

4. Repeat the words "lose time" to yourself over and over in your mind's voice to focus your perception. Continue repeating the words until you lose conscious awareness.

5. If you have a vivid dream where it seems like you are somewhere else in the room, think of exiting out of the nearest door to get as far away from where you fell asleep as possible.

Transcend Time

1. Relax as deeply as you can using the "Create a State of Focused Perception" practice.

2. Abruptly open your eyes and look around you.

3. Think this thought: *Everything is me.*

4. Hold this thought for as long as you can, even while your logical mind starts chattering.

5. As your thoughts drift, once again think this thought: *Everything is me.* Include everything around you in your thought: the chair, the computer, the desk, the book—everything.

6. See how long you can focus your mind before your brain begins to bombard you with thoughts that interrupt your focus. Use your will to reintroduce the idea that everything around you is you.

Advanced Technique: Enhancing the Experience

Look around you and imagine that everywhere you look you see yourself. There is no separation. Then imagine that you are seeing yourself in all that is around you and you are the creator of it. There may be boundaries you sense between you and, for instance, the table, but in some sense they are artificial. The atoms and subatomic particles that make up your body and the table are no different. Look deeper at your hand and at the table and imagine those boundaries do not exist.

Notes

Chapter 1: Time as We Know It

1. David Deming, "Do Extraordinary Claims Require Extraordinary Evidence?" *Philosophia* 44 (2016): 1319–31.

Chapter 2: One Part Physical

1. Albert Einstein, "On the Electrodynamics of Moving Bodies" [English translation of original 1905 German-language paper "Zur Elektrodynamik bewegter Korper," *Annalen der Physik* 322, no. 10 (1905): 891–921], *The Principle of Relativity* (London: Methuen and Co., Ltd., 1923), fourmilab.ch/etexts/einstein/specrel/specrel.pdf.

2. Albert Einstein, *Relativity: The Special and General Theory: A Popular Exposition*, trans. Robert W. Lawson, 3rd ed. (London: Methuen and Co., Ltd., 1916); Nola Taylor Redd, "Einstein's Theory of General Relativity," Space.com, November 7, 2017, space.com/17661-theory-general-relativity.html; Gene Kim and Jessica Orwig, "There Are 2 Types of Time Travel and Physicists Agree That One of Them Is Possible," *Business Insider*, November 21, 2017, businessinsider.com/how-to-time-travel-with -wormholes-2017-11.

3. Clara Moskowitz, "The Higher You Are, the Faster You Age," LiveScience, September 23, 2010, livescience.com/8672-higher-faster-age.html.

4. As an example, see Valtteri Arstila and Dan Lloyd, eds., *Subjective Time: The Philosophy, Psychology, and Neuroscience of Temporality* (Cambridge, MA: MIT Press, 2014).

5. Adrian Bejan, "Why the Days Seem Shorter as We Get Older," *European Review* 27, no. 2: 187–94, doi.org/10.1017 /S1062798718000741.

6. William Strauss and Neil Howe, *The Fourth Turning: What the Cycles of History Tell Us About Humanity's Next Rendezvous with Destiny* (New York: Broadway Books, 1997), 8–9.

7. The second law of thermodynamics states that when energy changes from one form to another, or when matter moves freely, entropy (a measurement of disorder) in a closed system increases. The result is that differences in things like temperature, pressure, and density tend to even out over time.

8. The science of thermodynamics, also called statistical mechanics.

9. Brian Greene, *Until the End of Time* (New York: Knopf, 2020), 23.

10. Greene, *Until the End of Time*, 35.

11. Albert Einstein and Nathan Rosen, "The Particle Problem in the General Theory of Relativity," *Physical Review* 48, no. 1 (1935): 73–77, doi.org/10.1103/physrev.48.73; "The Einstein-Rosen Bridge," Institute for Interstellar Studies, January 11, 2015, i4is .org/einstein-rosen-bridge; Kim and Orwig, "There Are 2 Types of Time Travel and Physicists Agree That One of Them Is Possible."

12. Werner Heisenberg, *Physics and Philosophy: The Revolution in Modern Science* (New York: Harper & Row, 1958); Roger Penrose, *The Road to Reality* (New York: Vintage, 2004), 523–24; Richard Feynman, *The Feynman Lectures on Physics*, Vol. III, 1–11, feynmanlectures.caltech.edu/III_01.html. Also, for an example of something that can plausibly happen but will likely take longer than the lifespan of the known universe, see Greene's example of the "Boltzmann brain," *Until the End of Time*, 297.

Chapter 3: One Part Perception

1. Natalie Wolchover, "What Is a Particle?" *Quanta Magazine*, November 12, 2020, quantamagazine.org/what-is-a-particle-20201112.

2. Subatomic particles, also called elementary particles, are the smallest and most basic constituents of matter (leptons and quarks) or are

combinations of these (hadrons, which consist of quarks), and those that transmit one of the four fundamental forces in nature (gravitational, electromagnetic, strong, and weak).

3. "Fundamental subatomic particles" include not just matter, but also "bosons"—the particles equivalent to the respective forces that affect matter, such as the photon, the vector bosons of the weak force, gluons for the strong nuclear force, and gravitons in gravity. These forces can be either particles or "fields" (e.g., the electromagnetic field or the gravitational field), which are closely related to "waves." Waves are simply modulations, or ripples, in a field. For example, an electromagnetic field from a broadcast antenna emits electromagnetic radiation, or waves, that can be picked up by a receiving antenna.

4. The "observer effect" is a term that has more widespread use than in just quantum theory. For example, when measuring anything, e.g., tire pressure or electrical voltage, the measurement affects the measured parameter. The term is also used in information theory.

5. As quoted in J. W. N. Sullivan, "Interviews with Great Scientists," *The Observer* (London, England), January 25, 1931, 17.

6. "NIST Team Proves 'Spooky Action at a Distance' Is Really Real," National Institute of Standards and Technology (NIST), November 10, 2015, nist.gov/news-events/news/2015/11/nist -team-proves-spooky-action-distance-really-real; study published as L. K. Shalm, E. Meyer-Scott, B. G. Christensen, P. Bierhorst, M. A. Wayne, D. R. Hamel, M. J. Stevens, et al., "A Strong Loophole-Free Test of Local Realism," *Physical Review Letters* 115, no. 25 (December 16, 2015): 250402, doi.org/10.1103 /PhysRevLett.115.250402.

7. Graham Hall, "Maxwell's Electromagnetic Theory and Special Relativity," *Philosophical Transactions of the Royal Society A* 366 (2008): 1849–60, doi.org/10.1098/rsta.2007.2192.

8. "Nobel Prize for Physics, 1979," *CERN Courier* (December): 395–97, cds.cern.ch/record/1730492/files/vol19-issue9-p395-e.pdf.

9. *Quantum uncertainty* describes the quantum behavior where we cannot know the speeds and positions of subatomic particles in the quantum world.

10. Leonard Susskind, "Copenhagen vs. Everett, Teleportation, and ER=EPR," lecture, April 23, 2016, Cornell University. doi.org/10 .1002/prop.201600036.

11. University of Vienna, "Quantum Gravity's Tangled Time," Phys.org, August 22, 2019, phys.org/news/2019-08-quantum-gravity -tangled.html.

12. H. Bösch, F. Steinkamp, and E. Boller, "Examining Psychokinesis: The Interaction of Human Intention with Random Number Generators—A Meta-Analysis," *Psychological Bulletin* 132 (2006): 497–523, doi.org/10.1037/0033-2909.132.4.497.

13. "Picturesque Speech and Patter," *Reader's Digest* 40 (April 1942): 92. Source verified by Quote Investigator, "Men Occasionally Stumble Over the Truth, But They Pick Themselves Up and Hurry Off," May 26, 2012, quoteinvestigator.com/2012/05/26 /stumble-over-truth/.

14. Christopher Chabris and Daniel Simons, "The Invisible Gorilla," accessed October 28, 2015, theinvisiblegorilla.com/gorilla _experiment.html.

Chapter 4: How the Unseen
Creates the Scene

1. Bonnie Horrigan, "Roger Nelson, PhD: The Global Consciousness Project," *EXPLORE* 2, no. 4 (July/August 2006): 343–51, doi.org /10.1016/j.explore.2006.05.012.

2. William G. Braud, "Distant Mental Influence of Rate of Hemolysis of Human Red Blood Cells," *Journal of the American Society for Psychical Research* 84, no. 1 (January 1990).

3. William Braud, *Distant Mental Influence: Its Contributions to Science, Consciousness, Healing and Human Interactions*, illustrated edition (Charlottesville, VA: Hampton Roads Publishing, 2003).

4. Braud, *Distant Mental Influence*.

5. William F. Russell, *Second Wind: The Memoirs of an Opinionated Man* (New York: Random House, 1979), 156–157.

6. Mihaly Csikszentmihalyi, *Flow: The Psychology of Optimal Experience* (New York: HarperCollins, 2009).

7. Fred Ovsiew, "The Zeitraffer Phenomenon, Akinetopsia, and the Visual Perception of Speed of Motion: A Case Report," *Neurocase* 20, no. 3 (June 2014): 269–72, doi.org/10.1080 /13554794.2013.770877.

8. R. Noyes and R. Kletti, "Depersonalization in Response to Life-Threatening Danger," *Comprehensive Psychiatry* 18 (1977): 375–84.

9. R. Noyes and R. Kletti, "The Experience of Dying from Falls," *Omega (Westport)* 3 (1972): 45–52.

10. Chess Stetson, Matthew P. Fiesta, and David M. Eagleman, "Does Time Really Slow Down during a Frightening Event?" *PLOS ONE* 2, no. 12 (2007): e1295, doi.org/10.1371/journal.pone.0001295.

11. Catalin V. Buhusi and Warren H. Meck, "What Makes Us Tick? Functional and Neural Mechanisms of Interval Timing," *National Review of Neuroscience* 6, no. 10 (October 2005): 755–65, doi.org /10.1038/nrn1764; Sylvie Droit-Volet, Sophie L. Fayolle, and Sandrine Gil, "Emotion and Time Perception: Effects of Film-Induced Mood," *Frontiers in Integrative Neuroscience* 5, no. 33 (August 2011), doi.org/10.3389/fnint.2011.00033.

12. Daniel C. Dennett and Marcel Kinsbourne, "Time and the Observer: The Where and When of Consciousness in the Brain," *Behavioral and Brain Sciences* 15 (1992): 183–247, ase.tufts.edu/cogstud/dennett /papers/Time_and_the_Observer.pdf.

13. Csikszentmihalyi, *Flow*.

Chapter 5: The Brainwave State
of Focused Perception

1. Neural pathways, made up of neurons connected by dendrites, are created in the brain based on our habits and behaviors.

2. Ned Herrmann, "What Is the Function of the Various Brainwaves?" *Scientific American*, December 22, 1997, scientificamerican.com /article/what-is-the-function-of-t-1997-12-22/.

3. A state of intense concentration achieved through meditation. In Hindu yoga, this is regarded as the ultimate stage of consciousness, at which union with the divine is reached (before or at death).

4. Marc Kaufman, "Meditation Gives Brain a Charge, Study Finds," *The Washington Post*, January 3, 2005, washingtonpost.com/archive /politics/2005/01/03/meditation-gives-brain-a-charge-study-finds /7edabb07-a035-4b20-aebc-16f4eac43a9e/.

5. Timothy J. Buschman, Eric L. Denovellis, Cinira Diogo, Daniel Bullock, and Earl K. Miller, "Synchronous Oscillatory Neural Ensembles for Rules in the Prefrontal Cortex," *Neuron* 76, no. 4 (November 21, 2012): 838–46, doi.org/10.1016 /j.neuron.2012.09.029.

6. Matthew P. A. Fisher, "Quantum Cognition: The Possibility of Processing with Nuclear Spins in the Brain," *Annals of Physics* 362 (November 2015): 593–602, doi.org/10.1016/j.aop.2015.08.020.

7. Jonathan O'Callaghan, "'Schrödinger's Bacterium' Could Be a Quantum Biology Milestone," *Scientific American*, October 29, 2018, scientificamerican.com/article/schroedingers-bacterium -could-be-a-quantum-biology-milestone/.

Chapter 6: Meditation

1. Judson A. Brewer, Patrick D. Worhunsky, Jeremy R. Gray, Yi-Yuan Tang, Jochen Weber, and Hedy Kober, "Meditation Experience Is Associated with Differences in Default Mode Network Activity and

Connectivity," *PNAS* 108, no. 50 (2011): 20254–59, doi.org/10
.1073/pnas.1112029108.

2. Eileen Luders, Nicolas Cherbuin, and Florian Kurth, "Forever
   Young(er): Potential Age-Defying Effects of Long-Term Mediation
   of Gray Matter Atrophy," *Frontiers in Psychology* 5, no. 1551
   (2015): doi.org/10.3389/fpsyg.2014.01551.

3. The term "hard problem of consciousness" was coined in 1995 by
   David Chalmers, an Australian philosopher and cognitive scientist
   researching the philosophies of mind and language.

4. Roger Penrose was awarded one-half of the 2020 Nobel Prize in
   Physics for his discovery that black hole formation is a prediction of
   the general theory of relativity.

5. Roger Penrose, *The Emperor's New Mind: Concerning Computers,
   Minds, and the Laws of Physics* (Oxford, England: Oxford Landmark
   Science, 2016).

6. University of Groningen, "Quantum Effects Observed in
   Photosynthesis," ScienceDaily, May 21, 2018, sciencedaily.com
   /releases/2018/05/180521131756.htm. For original journal article,
   see Erling Thyrhaug, Roel Tempelaar, Marcelo J. P. Alcocer, Karel
   Žídek, David Bína, Jasper Knoester, Thomas L. C. Jansen, and
   Donatas Zigmantas, "Identification and Characterization of Diverse
   Coherences in the Fenna–Matthews–Olson Complex," *Nature
   Chemistry* 10 (2018): 780–86, doi.org/10.1038/s41557-018-0060
   -5. Also see Hamish G. Hiscock, Susannah Worster, Daniel R.
   Kattnig, Charlotte Steers, Ye Jin, David E. Manolopoulos, Henrik
   Mouritsen, and P. J. Hore, "The Quantum Needle of the Avian
   Magnetic Compass," *PNAS* 113, no. 17 (2016): 4634–39, doi.org
   /10.1073/pnas.1600341113.

7. This practice is adapted from Gerald Epstein, *Encyclopedia of Mental
   Imagery: Colette Aboulker-Muscat's 2,100 Visualization Exercises
   for Personal Development, Healing, and Self-Knowledge*, illustrated
   edition (New York: ACMI Press, 2012).

Chapter 7: Imagination

1. Victoria Hazlitt, "Jean Piaget, the Child's Conception of Physical Causality," *The Pedagogical Seminary and Journal of Genetic Psychology* 40 (September 2012): 243–249, doi.org/10.1080 /08856559.1932.10534224.

2. Marie Buda, Alex Fornito, Zara M. Bergström, and Jon S. Simons, "A Specific Brain Structural Basis for Individual Differences in Reality Monitoring," *Journal of Neuroscience* 31, no. 40 (2011): 14308–13, doi.org/10.1523/JNEUROSCI.3595-11.2011.

3. L. Verdelle Clark, "Effect of Mental Practice on the Development of a Certain Motor Skill," *Research Quarterly of the American Association for Health, Physical Education & Recreation* 31 (1960): 560–69, psycnet.apa.org/record/1962-00248-001.

4. "Frequently Asked Questions," Program in Placebo Studies and Therapeutic Encounter (PiPS), Beth Israel Deaconess Medical Center/Harvard Medical School, programinplacebostudies.org /about/faq/.

5. Adapted from the work of bestselling author and speaker Marcia Wieder.

Chapter 8: Trauma

1. Roger E. Beaty, Paul Seli, and Daniel L. Schacter, "Thinking about the Past and Future in Daily Life: An Experience Sampling Study of Individual Differences in Mental Time Travel," *Psychological Research* 83, no. 8 (June 2019), doi.org/10.1007/s00426-018-1075-7.

2. Norman Doidge, *The Brain That Changes Itself* (New York: Penguin, 2008).

3. Zvi Carmeli and Rachel Blass, "The Case against Neuroplastic Analysis: A Further Illustration of the Irrelevance of Neuroscience to Psychoanalysis Through a Critique of Doidge's *The Brain That Changes Itself,*" *International Journal of Psychoanalysis* 94 (2013): 391–410, doi.org/10.1111/1745-8315.12022.

4. Victoria Follette, Kathleen M. Palm, and Adria N. Pearson, "Mindfulness and Trauma: Implications for Treatment," *Journal of Rational-Emotive and Cognitive-Behavior Therapy* 24, no. 1 (March 2006): 45–61, doi.org/10.1007/s10942-006-0025-2.

5. Yoon-Ho Kim, Rong Yu, Sergei P. Kulik, Yanhua Shih, and Marlan O. Scully, "A Delayed 'Choice' Quantum Eraser," *Physical Review Letters* 84, no. 1 (2000).

6. Vincent Jacques, E. Wu, Frédéric Grosshans, François Treussart, Philippe Grangier, Alain Aspect, and Jean-François Roch, "Experimental Realization of Wheeler's Delayed-Choice Gedanken Experiment," *Science* 315, no. 5814 (February 2007): 966–68, doi.org/10.1126/science.1136303.

7. Francesco Vedovato, Costantino Agnesi, Matteo Schiavon, Daniele Dequal, Luca Calderaro, Marco Tomasin, Davide G. Marangon, Andrea Stanco, Vincenza Luceri, Giuseppe Bianco, Giuseppe Vallone, and Paolo Villoresi, "Extending Wheeler's Delayed-Choice Experiment to Space," *Science Advances* 3, no. 10 (October 2017): e1701180, doi.org/10.1126/sciadv.1701180.

8. This practice is adapted from Gerald Epstein, *Encyclopedia of Mental Imagery: Colette Aboulker-Muscat's 2,100 Visualization Exercises for Personal Development, Healing, and Self-Knowledge*, illustrated edition (New York: ACMI Press, 2012).

Chapter 9: Worry

1. Bambi L. DeLaRosa, Jeffrey S. Spence, Scott K. M. Shakal, Michael A. Motes, Clifford S. Calley, Virginia I. Calley, John Hart Jr., and Michael A. Kraut, "Electrophysiological Spatiotemporal Dynamics During Implicit Visual Threat Processing," *Brain and Cognition* 91 (November 2014): 54–61, doi.org/10.1016/j.bandc.2014.08.003.

2. Charles Eisenstein, *The More Beautiful World Our Hearts Know Is Possible* (Berkeley, CA: North Atlantic Books, 2013), 244–47.

Chapter 10: Focus

1. Carlo Rovelli, *The Order of Time* (New York: Riverhead Books, 2018).

2. This description also suggests the block universe theory, a philosophical theory that states that the universe is a giant block of all the things that ever happened—including the past, present, and future—which exist all at once and are all equally real.

Chapter 11: Thoughts

1. Vivien Cumming, "The Other Person That Discovered Evolution, Besides Darwin," BBC online, November 7, 2016, bbc.com/earth /story/20161104-the-other-person-that-discovered-evolution -besides-darwin.

2. John B. West, "Carl Wilhelm Scheele, the Discoverer of Oxygen, and a Very Productive Chemist," *American Journal of Physiology: Lung Cellular and Molecular Physiology* 307, no. 11 (December 2014): L811–6, doi.org/10.1152/ajplung.00223.2014.

3. Stanley I. Sandler and Leslie V. Woodcock, "Historical Observations on Laws of Thermodynamics," *Journal of Chemical & Engineering Data* 55 (2010): 4485–90, doi.org/10.1021/je1006828.

4. "Georges Lemaître, Father of the Big Bang," American Museum of Natural History, amnh.org/learn-teach/curriculum-collections /cosmic-horizons-book/georges-lemaitre-big-bang. Excerpted from *Cosmic Horizons: Astronomy at the Cutting Edge*, Steven Soter and Neil deGrasse Tyson, eds. (New York: New Press, 2000).

5. *Proceedings of the American Academy of Arts and Sciences* 74, No. 6 (November 1940): 143–46.

6. Scott Camzine, Jena-Louis Deneubourg, Nigel R. Franks, James Sneyd, Guy Theraula, and Eric Bonabeau, *Self-Organization in Biological Systems* (Princeton, NJ: Princeton University Press, 2001), 7–14.

7. In physics, reductionism divides the world into basic building blocks for simplicity, while emergence seeks to come up with simple laws that come out of complexity.

8. Rupert Sheldrake, *A New Science of Life: The Hypothesis of Morphic Resonance* (Rochester, VT: Park Street Press, 1995).

9. Peter D. Bruza, Zheng Wang, and Jerome R. Busemeyer, "Quantum Cognition: A New Theoretical Approach to Psychology," *Trends in Cognitive Science* 19, no. 7 (July 2015): 383–93, doi.org/10.1016/j .tics.2015.05.001.

10. Filippo Caruso, "What Is Quantum Biology?" Lindau Nobel Laureate Meetings, June 15, 2016, lindau-nobel.org/what-is -quantum-biology/.

11. Matthew P. A. Fisher, "Quantum Cognition: The Possibility of Processing with Nuclear Spins in the Brain," *Annals of Physics* 362 (November 2015): 593–602, doi.org/10.1016/j.aop.2015.08.020.

12. David H. Freedman, "Quantum Consciousness," *Discover*, June 1, 1994, discovermagazine.com/mind/quantum-consciousness.

13. Berit Brogaard, "How Much Brain Tissue Do You Need to Function Normally?" *Psychology Today*, September 2, 2015, psychologytoday .com/us/blog/the-superhuman-mind/201509/how-much-brain -tissue-do-you-need-function-normally.

14. This practice is adapted from Gerald Epstein, *Encyclopedia of Mental Imagery: Colette Aboulker-Muscat's 2,100 Visualization Exercises for Personal Development, Healing, and Self-Knowledge*, illustrated edition (New York: ACMI Press, 2012).

Chapter 12: Telepathy

1. Carles Grau, Romuald Ginhoux, Alejandro Riera, Thanh Lam Nguyen, Hubert Chauvat, Michel Berg, Julià L. Amengual, Alvaro Pascual-Leone, Giulio Ruffini, "Conscious Brain-to-Brain Communication in

Humans Using Non-Invasive Technologies," *PLOS ONE* 9, no. 8 (August 19, 2014), doi.org/10.1371/journal.pone.0105225.

2. Ganesan Venkatasubramanian, Peruvumba N. Jayakumar, Hongasandra R. Nagendra, Dindagur Nagaraja, R. Deeptha, and Bangalore N. Gangadhar, "Investigating Paranormal Phenomena: Functional Brain Imaging of Telepathy," *International Journal of Yoga* 1, no. 2 (Jul–Dec. 2008): 66–71, ncbi.nlm.nih.gov/pmc /articles/PMC3144613/.

3. Doree Armstrong and Michelle Ma, "Researcher Controls Colleague's Motions in 1st Human Brain-to-Brain Interface," UW News, University of Washington, August 27, 2013, washington.edu/news /2013/08/27/researcher-controls-colleagues-motions-in-1st-human -brain-to-brain-interface/.

4. Peter Tompkins and Christopher Bird, *The Secret Life of Plants* (New York: Harper & Row, 1973). Also see Tristan Wang, "The Secret Life of Plants: Understanding Plant Sentience" [book review], *Harvard Science Review* (Fall 2013): harvardsciencereview.files .wordpress.com/2014/01/hsr-fall-2013-final.pdf.

5. C. Marletto, D. M. Coles, T. Farrow, and V. Vedral, "Entanglement between Living Bacteria and Quantized Light Witnessed by Rabi Splitting," *Journal of Physics Communication* 2, no. 10 (2018), doi .org/10.1088/2399-6528/aae224.

6. The "Bell test" refers to a test in which researchers measure correlations between the properties of pairs of photons. The timing of the measurement of the photons ensures that the correlations can't be explained by physical processes like preexisting conditions or the exchange of information at a rate less than the speed of light. Running statistical tests of these correlations are used to demonstrate that quantum mechanics is at work. This same phenomenon applies to any pair of entangled particles, not just photons.

7. Anil Ananthaswamy, "A Classic Quantum Test Could Reveal the Limits of the Human Mind," *NewScientist*, May 19, 2017,

newscientist.com/article/2131874-a-classic-quantum-test-could
-reveal-the-limits-of-the-human-mind/.

8. Peter G. Enticott, Hayley A. Kennedy, Nicole J. Rinehart, Bruce J. Tonge, John L. Bradshaw, John R. Taffe, Zafiris J. Daskalakis, and Paul B. Fitzgerald, "Mirror Neuron Activity Associated with Social Impairments but Not Age in Autism Spectrum Disorder," *Biological Psychiatry* 71, no. 5 (March 2012): 427–33, doi.org/10.1016/j .biopsych.2011.09.001.

9. Venkatasubramanian, et al., "Investigating Paranormal Phenomena: Functional Brain Imaging of Telepathy," 66–71.

Chapter 13: Supersight

1. Russell Targ and Harold Puthoff, "Remote Viewing of Natural Targets," Stanford Research Institute, to be presented at the Conference on Quantum Physics and Parapsychology, Geneva, Switzerland, August 26–27, 1974, cia.gov/readingroom/document /cia-rdp96-00787r000500410001-3.

2. Jim Schnabel, *Remote Viewers: The Secret History of America's Psychic Spies* (New York: Dell Publishing, 1997), 27.

3. Schnabel, *Remote Viewers*, 310.

4. Gabriel Popkin, "China's Quantum Satellite Achieves 'Spooky Action' at Record Distance," *Science*, June 15, 2017, sciencemag .org/news/2017/06/china-s-quantum-satellite-achieves-spooky -action-record-distance.

Chapter 14: Love

1. Jeff Wise, "When Fear Makes Us Superhuman," *Scientific American*, December 28, 2009, scientificamerican.com/article/extreme-fear -superhuman/. Excerpted from Jeff Wise, *Extreme Fear: The Science of Your Mind in Danger* (New York: Palgrave Macmillan, 2009).

2. Wise, "When Fear Makes Us Superhuman."

3. Meb Keflezighi with Scott Douglas, *26 Marathons: What I Learned about Faith, Identity, Running, and Life from My Marathon Career* (New York: Rodale, 2019).

4. Stephen E. Humphrey, Jennifer D. Nahrgang, and Frederick P. Morgeson, "Integrating Motivation, Social, and Contextual Work Design Features: A Meta-Analytic Summary and Theoretical Extension of the Work Design Literature," *Journal of Applied Psychology* 92, no. 5 (2007): 1332–56, doi.org/10.1037/0021-9010.92.5.1332.

5. Gary Zukav, "Love and Gravity," *HuffPost*, June 27, 2012, huffpost.com/entry/love_b_1457566.

6. Peter D. Bruza, Zheng Wang, and Jerome R. Busemeyer, "Quantum Cognition: A New Theoretical Approach to Psychology," *Trends in Cognitive Science* 19, no. 7 (July 2015): 383–93, doi.org/10.1016/j.tics.2015.05.001.

7. Sougato Bose, Anupam Mazumdar, Gavin W. Morley, Hendrik Ulbricht, Marko Toroš, Mauro Paternostro, Andrew A. Geraci, Peter F. Barker, M. S. Kim, and Gerard Milburn, "A Spin Entanglement Witness for Quantum Gravity," *Physical Review Letters* 119, no. 24 (2017): 240401, doi.org/10.1103/PhysRevLett.119.240401.

8. Marcelo Gleiser, *The Simple Beauty of the Unexpected: A Natural Philosopher's Quest for Trout and the Meaning of Everything* (Lebanon, NH: ForeEdge, 2016).

9. This practice is adapted from Drunvalo Melchizedek.

Chapter 15: Death

1. Stephan Schwartz, "Crossing the Threshold: Nonlocal Consciousness and the Burden of Proof," *EXPLORE: The Journal of Science and Healing* 9, no. 2: 77–81, pubmed.ncbi.nlm.nih.gov/23452708/.

2. Stuart Youngner and Insoo Hyun, "Pig Experiment Challenges Assumptions around Brain Damage in People," *Nature*, April 17, 2019, nature.com/articles/d41586-019-01169-8.

3. Andra M. Smith and Claude Messier, "Voluntary Out-of-Body Experience: An fMRI Study," *Frontiers in Human Neuroscience* 8 (February 2014), doi.org/10.3389/fnhum.2014.00070.

4. University College London, "First Out-of-Body Experience Induced in Laboratory Setting," Science News, *ScienceDaily*, August 24, 2007, sciencedaily.com/releases/2007/08/070823141057.htm. Journal article available at H. Henrik Ehrsson, "The Experimental Induction of Out-of-Body Experiences," *Science* 317, no. 5841 (2007): 1048, doi.org/10.1126/science.1142175.

5. Christopher French, "Near-Death Experiences in Cardiac Arrest Survivors," *Progress in Brain Research* 150 (2005): 351–67, doi.org/10.1016/S0079-6123(05)50025-6.

6. Larry Dossey, "Spirituality and Nonlocal Mind: A Necessary Dyad," *Spirituality in Clinical Practice* 1, no. 1 (2014) 29–42, doi.org/10.1037/scp0000001.

7. William Buhlman, "The Life-Changing Benefits Reported from Out-of-Body Experiences," The Monroe Institute, monroeinstitute.org/blogs/blog/the-life-changing-benefits-reported-from-out-of-body-experiences, accessed February 20, 2021.

8. Stephen LaBerge, Kristen LaMarca, and Benjamin Baird, "Pre-Sleep Treatment with Galantamine Stimulates Lucid Dreaming: A Double-Blind, Placebo-Controlled, Crossover Study," *PLOS ONE* 13, no. 8 (2018): e0201246, doi.org/10.1371/journal.pone.0201246.

Chapter 16: Immortality

1. Jim B. Tucker, *Return to Life: Extraordinary Cases of Children Who Remember Past Lives* (New York: St. Martin's Press, 2013), 1–12.

2. Robert Lawrence Kuhn, "Forget Space-Time: Information May Create the Cosmos," Space.com, May 23, 2015, space.com/29477 -did-information-create-the-cosmos.html.

3. Roger Penrose and Stuart Hameroff, "Consciousness in the Universe: Neuroscience, Quantum Space-Time Geometry and Orch OR Theory," *Journal of Cosmology* 14 (2011): 1–17, journalofcosmology.com/Consciousness160.html.

4. Jharana Rani Samal, Arun K. Pati, and Anil Kumar, "Experimental Test of the Quantum No-Hiding Theorem," *Physical Review Letters* 106, no. 8 (2011): 080401, doi.org/10.1103/PhysRevLett .106.080401.

5. Erwin Schrödinger, *What Is Life?* (Cambridge, UK: Cambridge University Press, 1967, first edition 1944). Based on lectures delivered under the auspices of the Dublin Institute for Advanced Studies at Trinity College, Dublin, February 1943.

Appendix A: Additional Science

1. Recall the first such experiment using light was done by Thomas Young in the classical physics world of 1803. Later on, Clinton Davisson and Lester Germer extended the double-slit experiment to the quantum world around 1927 using electrons, which are quantum particles.

2. Markus Arndt, Olaf Nairz, Julian Vos-Andreae, Claudia Keller, Gerbrand van der Zouw, and Anton Zeilinger, "Wave-Particle Duality of C60 Molecules," *Nature* 401 (1999): 680–82, doi.org/10.1038/44348.

3. Brian Greene, *The Fabric of the Cosmos* (New York: Vintage, 2005): 197–204. Also see Marlan Scully and Kai Druhl, "Quantum Eraser: A Proposed Photon Correlation Experiment Concerning Observation and 'Delayed Choice' in Quantum Mechanics," *Physical Review A* 25 (April 1, 1982): 2208.

4. Richard Conn Henry, "The Mental Universe," *Nature* (July 6, 2005): doi.org/10.1038/436029a.

5. Brookhaven National Laboratory, "Research Team Expands Quantum Network with Successful Long-Distance Entanglement Experiment," Phys.org, April 8, 2019, phys.org/news/2019-04 -team-quantum-network-successful-long-distance.html.

6. Leonard Susskind, "Copenhagen vs. Everett, Teleportation, and ER=EPR," lecture, April 23, 2016, Cornell University, doi.org/10 .1002/prop.201600036.

7. University of Vienna, "Quantum Gravity's Tangled Time," Phys.org, August 22, 2019, phys.org/news/2019-08-quantum-gravity-tangled.html.

8. University of Vienna, "Quantum Gravity's Tangled Time."

9. H. Bösch, F. Steinkamp, E. Boller, "Examining Psychokinesis: The Interaction of Human Intention with Random Number Generators—A Meta-Analysis," *Psychological Bulletin* 132 (2006): 497–523, doi.org/10.1037/0033-2909.132.4.497.

10. D. I. Radin and R. D. Nelson, "Evidence for Consciousness-Related Anomalies in Random Physical Systems," *Foundations of Physics* 19 (1989): 1499–514, doi.org/10.1007/BF00732509.

11. D. Davidenko, *Ich denke, also Bin Ich: Descartes Ausschweifendes Leben* [English: *I Am Thinking, Therefore I Am: Descartes's Excessive Life*] (Frankfurt: Eichborn, 1990).

12. J. B. Rhine, "'Mind over Matter' or the PK Effect," *Journal of American Society for Psychical Research* 38 (1944): 185–201.

13. W. von Lucadou and H. Römer, "Synchronistic Phenomena as Entanglement Correlations in Generalized Quantum Theory," *Journal of Consciousness Studies* 14 (2007): 50–74.

14. Roger Penrose and Stuart Hameroff, "Consciousness in the Universe: Neuroscience, Quantum Space-Time Geometry, and Orch OR Theory," *Journal of Cosmology* 14 (2011): 1–17, journalofcosmology.com/Consciousness160.html.

Appendix B: A Compilation of Practices

1. This practice is adapted from Gerald Epstein, *Encyclopedia of Mental Imagery: Colette Aboulker-Muscat's 2,100 Visualization Exercises for Personal Development, Healing, and Self-Knowledge*, illustrated edition (New York: ACMI Press, 2012).

2. This practice is adapted from Gerald Epstein, *Encyclopedia of Mental Imagery*.

3. This practice is adapted from Charles Eisenstein, *The More Beautiful World Our Hearts Know Is Possible* (Berkeley, CA: North Atlantic Books, 2013), 244–47.

4. This practice is adapted from Gerald Epstein, *Encyclopedia of Mental Imagery*.

5. This practice is adapted from Drunvalo Melchizedek.

About the Author

With her aptitude for making science understandable, relevant, and captivating, Lisa Broderick helps others shift their understanding and make profound changes in their lives. For over four decades, she has worked with entrepreneurs as well as established professionals and companies. Her approach of integrating science with metaphysics and her own personal experiences has helped countless others lead lives of purpose and presence by reimagining how they see themselves and their businesses and how the world sees them.

Earlier in her life, Lisa earned a BA from Stanford University and an MBA from Duke and started a career as a business and finance consultant. Today, Lisa's passion is helping others with little or no scientific or spiritual training master their innate abilities with practices designed to improve their lives, their relationships, and the world.

She also uses her teaching and skills to guide the nonprofit she founded, Police2Peace. Police2Peace was formed to reimagine how the police see themselves and how the community sees them using the term "peace officer." As a national nonpartisan, not-for-profit corporation, Police2Peace unites communities and police services around solutions that uplift and heal them. Lisa is also a member of Rotary International, Mediators Beyond Borders International, the United Nations Association, the Alliance for Peacebuilding, and Women in Technology, and volunteers as a board member of the Relationship Foundation for Trauma-Informed Curriculum and the Save an Animal Foundation. Lisa is an amateur jazz musician and enjoys teaching students of all ages.

About Sounds True

Sounds True is a multimedia publisher whose mission is to inspire and support personal transformation and spiritual awakening. Founded in 1985 and located in Boulder, Colorado, we work with many of the leading spiritual teachers, thinkers, healers, and visionary artists of our time. We strive with every title to preserve the essential "living wisdom" of the author or artist. It is our goal to create products that not only provide information to a reader or listener but also embody the quality of a wisdom transmission.

For those seeking genuine transformation, Sounds True is your trusted partner. At SoundsTrue.com you will find a wealth of free resources to support your journey, including exclusive weekly audio interviews, free downloads, interactive learning tools, and other special savings on all our titles.

To learn more, please visit SoundsTrue.com/freegifts or call us toll-free at 800.333.9185.